YES, YOU CAN STILL RETIRE COMFORTABLY!

ALSO BY BEN STEIN

THE GIFT OF PEACE

HOW SUCCESSFUL PEOPLE WIN

HOW TO RUIN YOUR FINANCIAL LIFE

HOW TO RUIN YOUR LIFE hardcover (also available as an audio book)

HOW TO RUIN YOUR LOVE LIFE

HOW TO RUIN YOUR LIFE
(tradepaper, which comprises the three HOW TO RUIN titles above)

THE REAL STARS: In Today's America, Who Are the True Heroes?

26 STEPS TO SUCCEED IN HOLLYWOOD (with Al Burton)

WHAT YOUR KIDS NEED TO KNOW ABOUT MONEY AND SUCCESS

■ ■ ■

BY BEN STEIN AND PHIL DEMUTH

*CAN AMERICA SURVIVE?: The Rage of the Left,
the Truth, and What to Do about It*

HOW TO RUIN THE UNITED STATES OF AMERICA

*YES, YOU CAN BE A SUCCESSFUL INCOME INVESTOR!:
Reaching for Yield in Today's Market*

*YES, YOU CAN GET A FINANCIAL LIFE!:
Your Lifetime Guide to Financial Planning*

*YES, YOU CAN SUPERCHARGE YOUR PORTFOLIO!:
Six Steps for Investing Success in the 21st Century*

■ ■ ■

All of the above are available at your local bookstore,
or may be ordered by visiting:

Hay House USA: **www.hayhouse.com**
Hay House Australia: **www.hayhouse.com.au**
Hay House UK: **www.hayhouse.co.uk**
Hay House South Africa: **www.hayhouse.co.za**

YES, YOU CAN STILL RETIRE COMFORTABLY!

THE BABY-BOOM RETIREMENT CRISIS AND HOW TO BEAT IT

BEN STEIN AND PHIL DeMUTH

NBP

NEW BEGINNINGS PRESS
Carlsbad, California

Published by: New Beginnings Press, Carlsbad, California

Distributed in the United States by: Hay House, Inc.: www.hayhouse.com • *Distributed in Australia by:* Hay House Australia Pty. Ltd.: www.hayhouse.com.au • *Distributed in the United Kingdom by:* Hay House UK, Ltd.: www.hayhouse.co.uk • *Distributed in the Republic of South Africa by:* Hay House SA (Pty), Ltd.: www.hayhouse.co.za • *Distributed in Canada by:* Raincoast: www.raincoast.com • *Distributed in India by:* Hay House Publishers India: www.hayhouse.co.in

Editorial supervision: Jill Kramer   *Design:* Tricia Breidenthal

Library of Congress Cataloging-in-Publication Data

Stein, Benjamin, 1944-
  Yes, you can still retire comfortably! : the baby-boom retirement crisis and how to beat it / Ben Stein and Phil DeMuth.
    p. cm.
  Includes index.
  ISBN-13: 978-1-4019-0318-3 (hardcover)
  ISBN-10: 1-4019-0318-5 (tradepaper)
  ISBN-13: 978-1-4019-0317-6 (hardcover)
  ISBN-10: 1-4019-0317-7
  1. Older people--Finance, Personal. 2. Retirement--United States--Planning. 3. Retirement income--United States. 4. Baby boom generation--United States--Retirement. 5. Baby boom generation--United States--Economic conditions. I. DeMuth, Phil, 1950- II. Title.
  HG179.S8314 2005
  332.024'014--dc22

                                        2005004740

Hardcover ISBN 13: 978-1-4019-0318-5
Hardcover ISBN 10: 1-4019-0318-5
Tradepaper ISBN 13: 978-1-4019-0317-7
Tradepaper ISBN 10: 1-4019-0317-7

11 10 09 08   6 5 4 3
1st printing, August 2005
3rd printing, March 2008

Printed in the United States of America

For our generation

Contents

Introduction

Money is an astonishingly powerful mind changer. Lots of it—or at least enough of it—makes you happy, while a shortage makes you miserable. There's some magic to having enough that's as basic as the need to take in water and oxygen. The "mojo" of having *more* than enough, of having an amount necessary to be comfortable, is intoxicating.

Just think about how you feel when you open a brokerage statement that says your investments have been doing well, and compare that with how you feel when it says they've been doing poorly. Imagine what it means to open an envelope and find a check instead of a bill.

Years ago, one of your authors, Ben Stein, got a call asking him to do a commercial for which he was to be paid what seemed like a lordly sum. He had lunch with a friend right after he took the call, and his friend asked if he'd had a face-lift. "No," Ben replied, "I just got offered a lot of money to do something pleasant and easy."

"Money," she said sagely, "can make you look younger. Or," she added ruefully (because she was short of money), "it can age you."

We, your authors, are just ordinary people like you. We worry about money all the time, and whether we have enough of it. As we get older, we're concerned about whether we've invested wisely. (We often haven't, but we're getting better with age . . . we hope.) Most of all, we think about whether we'll have enough to live comfortably when we're too old and infirm—or just too worn-out—to work, and whether the people we love will have enough. We've seen magnificent examples of retirement preparedness—especially in our parents, all of whom died far too young—but we've also seen disasters among people we're very close to.

This has prompted very serious study on our part to save ourselves and others. We want to begin our salvation at home, but we'd like to spare as many people as possible sleepless nights and torment. We love this country more than words can say, and we're devoted to our fellow American citizens, as well as those of the UK, Canada, and all good countries. We want to offer some help based on our own terrible experiences and terrifying observations, as well as what we've seen that works. That help is within these pages. If you read and learn from it, your chances for a successful retirement will rise markedly.

As you make your way through this book, please bear in mind an admonition from a famous 12-step program: "No one among us has been able to maintain anywhere near perfect adherence to these principles." Like the organizations that save lives from alcohol and drugs, this program is meant to be suggestive and to provoke thought. The closer you can come to doing the actions we suggest after thinking it over, the better off you'll be.

We've seen the future, and it scares us; we've seen the past, in our parents' prudent behavior, and it was inspiring. One of your authors (yep, Ben Stein again) especially saw spectacular results in his parents' lives from the regular purchase of carefully selected variable annuities (VAs) in stocks. If we harp on regular purchases and on VAs, it's because we've seen that they work miracles when carefully chosen and well understood. If you notice our emphasis on diversification, you can rest assured that we've also seen that practice achieve wonderful success. Above all, if we can teach you that a little self-discipline from a young age can transform your future by allowing the passage of time and compound interest to do the heavy lifting, we will have justified the few shekels you spent on this book.

Please take care not to torture yourself as you read if you've been way off course so far. Believe us, we've made every mistake possible. But each day starts a new wave of possibility, and we hope that you can ride that wave into a glorious, golden sunset. If you have any problems with the math and research here, e-mail Phil DeMuth. He did all the hard work for this volume (and if Phil finds that he has made any dumb mistakes, he'll post corrections on our Website, **www.stein-demuth.com**). If you want someone to come over and babysit your German shorthaired pointer, e-mail Ben.

■ ■ ■

PART I

YES, YOU CAN STILL RETIRE COMFORTABLY!*

*But Not Everyone Will Be So Lucky . . .

The 21 Basic Rules of Retirement

1. Maximize your abilities through self-discipline and the ability to get along with others.

2. Start saving early. If it doesn't hurt, you're probably not saving enough.

3. Never spend more than you earn.

4. Max out all your retirement plans every year.

5. Get and stay married to a sensible person.

6. Buy your home.

7. Plan far ahead for your retirement, and then stick to your program.

8. Make a plan with a reliable financial adviser. Don't be afraid to ask for advice.

9. Save your hindquarters, not your face—that is, make savings and financial stability more important than showing off or looking cool.

10. Adopt a straightforward investment philosophy that takes advantage of the historical benefits of investing

in common stocks but balances it with bonds in a judicious mixture.

11. Don't swing for the fences. You'll get into good retirement shape with singles and walks—in other words, don't try for something brilliant. Just stay even with the market and you'll do great.

12. Always have a reserve of cash on hand so that you don't have to dig deeply into your stock-and-bond savings.

13. At the earliest possible stage of life, learn to enjoy yourself in some other way than impoverishing yourself or beggaring your retirement plan.

14. Acquire work skills that are in demand so that you'll consistently be employed and won't need to use up your savings while unemployed.

15. If you're starting a business, make someone else put up the money while you put up the sweat.

16. Consider the tax implications of everything you do.

17. Planning for your retirement is more important than offering a lavish life to your children. They're young and strong and can fend for themselves.

18. Know in your heart that you'll be fine if you err by having too much savings—*not* if you have too little.

19. Be able to say no to people who ask for money, even if they have the same last name as you.

4

20. Make sure your plan allows for flexibility if economic times and styles change, but don't follow fads or trends.

21. Keep in mind that no matter what, you don't want to be old, weak, ill, and poor.

■ ■ ■

Retirement Planning Decade by Decade

Teenage Years

- Study hard so that you can get into the best possible college or trade school.

- Learn the habit of working and earning to pay for what you want and need, not whining and moaning about it to your parents.

- Learn a hobby that will keep you occupied without spending a vast amount of money: Listening to opera or classic rock, carefully perusing the newspapers, and reading history are some examples.

- Get the most basic primers on stock- and bond-market strategy and start reading them carefully, but don't expect to understand them right away—no one ever does.

- Keep a small savings and stock market account just for the purpose of learning and developing good habits.

- Don't smoke or use drugs.

- Don't drink to excess.

Twenties

College Years

- Pay for as much of your education as is necessary through your own labor so that you learn the habit of connecting effort with reward.

- Study as hard as you can so that you can get into the best possible graduate school and secure the best possible job. Employers and admissions officers are sensitive to dips in your academic record.

- If possible, let your savings account grow, and add to it by working.

- Learn more about the stock market and about investing.

8

Post-School

- Do your best at your job. Employers are keenly aware of who's trying and who isn't. Learn as many of the skills of your career as fast as you can.

- Make your colleagues into friends. All advancement comes from a combination of ability and *aff*ability.

- Add to your savings as much as possible.

- Create a retirement plan with sufficient flexibility to adapt to what will likely be job and even career changes. This means having your own retirement account right away.

- Take part in all tax-advantaged, employer-subsidized savings plans, such as Keoghs and 401(k)s.

- Max out all such contributions.

- Start saving, using the rates we recommend as an absolute minimum level. Every dollar you set aside now grows geometrically thanks to compound interest.

- Credit cards are like nitroglycerine: Handle with care.

Thirties

- If at all possible, buy your own house, and eventually, a vacation home as well. People who own their homes are natural savers.

- If you're handy and have extra time, consider buying rental property.

- Continue to add to your skill sets as you see the economy changing and evolving, so you stand in the intersection of where society is going.

- Add to your tax-advantaged savings accounts whenever you can to the maximum extent allowed by law.

- Add to your employer-subsidized accounts as much as possible.

- Take a course in the stock market at the local junior college, and read the annual reports of Berkshire Hathaway online. If you haven't already done so, begin what we call a "couch potato portfolio" of 50 percent total stock market index and 50 percent total bond market index, available from any large broker or mutual fund company at low expense. (We give a full explanation of this portfolio in Chapter 4.)

9

- Once your tax-advantaged accounts are maxed out, begin a monthly or quarterly program of building a variable annuity account, after shopping carefully for the most advantageous rates.

- Develop new hobbies that don't require the expenditure of large sums of money.

- Stay off the conspicuous consumption treadmill.

- Every five years, check your savings against our recommended amounts to make sure you're on track, and adjust your course as needed.

- A couple of hours spent with a fee-only certified financial planner will do wonders for your life.

10

Forties

- Continue to add to your work skills and develop your aptitudes.

- Max out IRAs, Keoghs, and 401(k)s and add to variable annuities and any other tax-advantaged accounts.

- Pay more than the minimum on your home mortgage with the view of getting it down to zero by the time you retire.

- Keep track of your well-being and seek to remain in as good health as possible.

- If you're married, stay that way if at all possible. This can be a time of severe marital stress. Try to get through it by prayer and working at common interests. The economic consequences of divorce, except in rare cases, are seriously disadvantageous.

- Continue to add to your couch potato account of 50 percent total stock market index, 50 percent bond market index. Maintain a meaningful cash position as well so that you don't need to dip in to stock accounts for eventualities.

- At age 45, do a reality checkup to see where you stand vis-à-vis retirement. Don't hesitate to get professional help if you need it.

- Of course you have a will, don't you?

Fifties

- Follow the same methodologies and actions as in your 40s, except add as much as possible to the couch potato portfolio. This will be your maximum decade for adding to savings if you follow standard practices.

- Stay married—love the one you're with.

- Maintain even better health, because at this point, it becomes close to synonymous with wealth.

- Consider what skills you have that you might be able to utilize in a part-time career after retirement.

- As you travel for business, keep mental notes on places that might be suitable to relocate to after you retire.

- Make sure your savings are growing on course.

- Develop hobbies and activities that you can practice post-retirement.

- This is a good time to consider buying long-term-care insurance, especially if you're neither rich enough to self-insure nor poor enough to be taken care of by the state.

Sixties

Pre-retirement

- Start rebalancing your couch potato portfolio every year, preferably when you add new money.

- When you get within five years of retirement, start shunting new money into the real estate investment trusts and high-dividend stocks.

- Use Intuit's Quicken or Microsoft's Money software for a year to get a fix on your probable post-retirement expenses. Don't forget to budget for big-ticket items like cars and home-maintenance expenses (such as a new roof, plumbing, or furnace) that occur infrequently but are expensive when they hit. Don't forget Medicare and Medigap insurance premiums either, as well as out-of-pocket medical services not covered by these plans.

- Set up a post-retirement career if at all possible. Get it up and running while you still have a paycheck so that there aren't any unpleasant surprises later.

- The later you stop working, the better for your retirement finances.

At Retirement

- Use our tables and worksheets to determine your initial safe-withdrawal levels.

- Set up your income portfolio and arrange to electronically sweep the coupons and dividends into your bank account every quarter.

- Tell Social Security that you want payments to begin (this doesn't happen automatically).

- In addition to everything else, you'll need an emergency fund that isn't part of your nest egg. This should contain enough cash to get you through several months' worth of expenses. Both you and your spouse need to be on the account so that either one of you can access the money if needed.

- Unless you have a government pension or one with a cost-of-living adjustment, consider taking a lump-sum payout (in whatever form makes sense, taxwise) and either adding the proceeds to your portfolio or using them to buy an immediate annuity.

- Roll over your 401(k) with its dismal menu of choices and its high fees to an IRA at Vanguard, Fidelity, or another low-cost provider with a good selection of low-expense index funds.

- If necessary, annuitize your nest egg, take out a reverse mortgage, and/or relocate to an area with a lower cost of living.

In Retirement

- Make sure your estate plan is in good order.

- Don't forget to set up living wills and durable powers of attorney.

- Create a letter with instructions for the spouse who doesn't normally handle the finances, including the locations of all the accounts, statements, policies, tax returns, and keys to the safe-deposit box; phone numbers of accountants, brokers, insurance agents, and attorneys; account passwords; and so on.

- Anything you can do in early retirement to provide an income stream will take that much weight off of your nest egg.

- Adjust the withdrawal from your couch potato portfolio every year by the rate of inflation.

- If your nest egg is down 10 percent only a few years after retirement, perhaps due to excessive withdrawals or falling markets, it's time to tighten your belt, no matter what the tables say.

- Every five years, recalculate your retirement withdrawals as if you were starting anew.

Seventies and Beyond

- Begin taking your required substantially equal IRA distributions by the time you're age 70½.

- Keep your letter of emergency instructions updated as conditions change.

- Do your children know that you love them? If not, when were you planning on telling them?

- Whom do you need to set things right with? Now might be a good time.

- Every five years, recalibrate your nest egg withdrawal rate according to our tables.

- Every five years, check the yield on your income account and match it to your couch potato account if needed.

- Rebalance your accounts only when needed.

■ ■ ■

CHAPTER 1

The Coming Baby-Boom Retirement Crisis

A specter is haunting the baby boomers: the specter of retirement. As with a python that swallowed a goat, the baby-boom demographic is a giant lump moving through the economic system, and it's now on the cusp of retirement. A generation of 78 million Americans stands largely unprepared.

When the crisis is actually upon us, you'll read human-interest stories in the newspapers about people who once seemed to be well-off, but who now have nothing and don't know what to do. And actually, you won't even need to read about it in the papers, because their numbers will include your friends. The press will frame this as a cautionary tale, an updated Aesop's fable of the grasshopper (played here by the self-indulgent, make-a-dollar, spend-a-dollar baby boomers) and the ant (those few who were wise and frugal enough to prepare). But, in truth, it's only partly a morality play—it's also a matter of demographic inevitability.

Retirement is traditionally said to rest upon a three-legged stool. The three legs are: Social Security, your pension benefits, and your personal savings. Let's look at it piece by piece in order to see how sturdy this stool is upon which your future rests. Prepare to be frightened.

Leg One: Benefits from the Government

The first thing you need to know is that your personal Social Security savings don't reside in a numbered safe-deposit box behind a heavy vault door in Washington, D.C. It would be nice to think that the government safely stows all the cash you pay in every year, putting it away to earn interest on your behalf, but the reality is decidedly otherwise. Social Security is a "pay-as-you-go" system: The government takes the money from your paycheck today *and* spends it today, doling it out to current retirees—in fact, paying them vastly more than they ever put into the system. Al Gore's prattle about putting a "lockbox" on the Social Security trust fund was either doltishly naïve or cruelly cynical, because there's no box to put a lock on. It's accounting fiction. He might as well have suggested that we keep the money in Uncle Scrooge McDuck's money bin.

When the demographic lump of baby boomers first started moving through the system in the 1960s and 1970s, and even up through the present, there was no problem with this arrangement. The boomers provided lots and lots of workers paying into Social Security to fund the retirements of those few individuals a little bit ahead of them.

In a few years, however—beginning in earnest in 2008, when the first wave of boomers reaches age 62 and becomes eligible for Social Security—this demographic lump itself will all be retired. Then there will be comparatively fewer workers (those left in the "python" a bit behind the boomers) paying into the system, and at that point, the pay-as-you-go model begins to disintegrate.

In reality, it's already broken down, and a giant stack of IOUs is accumulating that will come due to your children. Add in Medicare expenditures, and far from having a surplus, you're already devoting 3.6 percent of personal and corporate tax revenues to meet the shortfall from Social Security and Medicare taxes today. By 2030, this shortage will require 52.7 percent of general tax revenues, and by 2070, they'll need 100 percent, according to the National Center for Policy Analysis. At that point, action will be essential, since this doesn't leave any money to pay Congress's salary.

What really exists is a two-part problem: Too many people about to retire (thanks to the postwar baby boom), and too few workers to subsidize their (prolonged and ever-more-expensive) retirements. Instead of 7.3 workers per retiree, as there were in 1950, or 4.7 each, as there are now; in 2035, there will only be 2.7 individuals in the workforce for each Social Security recipient. All in all, the burden per worker will go up 74 percent from today, even if the costs remain constant—which they won't. Costs are rising astronomically. Something has to give.

In 1935, when Social Security got started, the average male worker didn't even live to age 65 (just as black males still don't survive to that age, on average). Cigarettes, by killing off large numbers of the population prematurely, were a tremendous asset to the system. Today's retirees, however, live about 17 years longer than the ones back then. Yet over the decades, the minimum retirement age for Social Security benefits has only advanced by a total of one year.

It was never intended that Americans should work for 44 years and then retire and be supported (by whom?) for 23 more years after that, prior to shuffling off this mortal coil. Yet this has been promoted into the *routine* expectation. Worse still, most people would prefer to take an *early* retirement.

Meanwhile, this looming crisis doesn't even appear on the books of the U.S. government. Social Security and Medicare, which provide income and medical benefits to retirees, presently account for more than one-third of all federal spending. In fact, Congress recently authorized a vast expansion of these benefits to include prescription drugs. Unfortunately, it didn't see its way to providing any method to pay for this largesse. It charged a $7.5 trillion gift to taxpayers, putting the bill on a credit card that they lent it, and this debt is going to come due to a future generation. Politicians have pandered to older voters today by placing an inconceivably massive, but invisible (for the present) financial burden on people who can't lift a finger to protest: the young and the unborn—in other words, on your children.

How big is the bill that's coming for Social Security and Medicare? The sum of future obligations Congress has promised (as of October 2004, courtesy of economists Jagadeesh Gokhale and Kent Smetters) totals *$72.4 trillion.* To break it down: $10.4 trillion is for Social Security, and $62 trillion is for Medicare. This is the amount of money we'd need in the bank earning interest today to cover our future liabilities. And this amount is rising every day.

How much is $72.4 trillion? Sure, it sounds like a lot of money, but is it really? Lets put this amount in context: At the start of 2000, the total equity value of all publicly traded companies in the world was $36.1 trillion; the value of every bond in the world was $31 trillion.

So even if you owned the entire global stock and bond markets, you wouldn't have enough money in the bank to pay for Social Security and Medicare—you'd still be $5.3 trillion short, and to some people, even this paltry sum is a lot of money. The entire amount that Americans owe on their houses, cars, and credit cards totals about $9.5 trillion; the entire amount that they have in their IRAs is $2.6 trillion; and the combined worth of all of the nation's public and private pension funds is about $6 trillion.

Bill Gates is widely reputed to be a rich man—the richest in the world, in fact. His net worth is some $29.4 billion, based on today's Microsoft stock price. But the amount of money needed to pay for the unfunded Social Security and Medicare liability is 2,470 times as much money as Bill has.

Here's yet another way of looking at the size of the obligation: It's more than six times the total value of every good produced and service sold in the United States in 2004.

Americans are living in a dreamland. The median taxpayers today, a married working couple earning $46,400 a year, will have paid into the system a total of $198,000 in Social Security taxes and $43,400 in Medicare taxes. Then they'll pull out a sum of $326,000 in Social Security and $283,500 in Medicare benefits (all these figures are in present dollars). The difference—$328,200—is the burden being shifted to future taxpayers . . . and that's just one average couple. In reality, the entire $609,500 will have to come from future taxpayers, because the money this couple paid has already been spent. It's gone.

In short, our government is running a gigantic Ponzi scheme, using the money coming in to pay off the first investors, not investing the money on behalf of current payers, and the situation is unsustainable. As economist Herbert Stein pointed out, if a trend can't continue forever, it will stop. It will end in tears.

What Can Be Done?

There are two quick solutions for the government:

1. Don't pay the money.
2. Do pay the money, but pay it with worthlessly inflated dollars.

Congress has made a promise, and it can break its word. By changing the law, voters can get rid of this crushing obligation at the stroke of a pen. But while this "solves" the problem, it does so by hanging senior citizens out to dry.

Alternatively, by running its printing presses at full tilt, the government could produce money with a lot of zeroes on it and settle the debt at once. A single bill with a number followed by 12 zeroes could cover the entire cost, but this would both leave seniors in the lurch *and* destroy the economy.

Both of these approaches are politically unpalatable. Unfortunately, the next round of solutions is also tough to swallow and guaranteed to be unpopular.

3. Raise the relevant federal taxes immediately (roughly double them).
4. Cut benefits immediately (roughly in half).
5. Some combination of the above.

These options are hardly trouble-free. For example, taxing your way out of the hole could involve raising taxes to a point that would discourage work and suppress economic output, and give rise to an even larger gray-market economy (with its attendant disrespect for law). Cutting benefits in half could produce legions of seniors begging in the streets. Either way, profound social dislocations of one sort or another would follow.

One solution often touted is for everyone to start saving aggressively. The problem is that the resulting drop in consumption would likely trigger a recession or a full-blown depression. In the extremely unlikely event that everyone in the baby-boom generation did save, you'd still be faced with the problem later of a large group of retirees trading the sum total of its assets for goods and services from a much smaller labor force. This would either depress the value of the assets being sold, or inflate the prices of the goods and services that seniors want (or both), but in either event offsetting the benefit of their earlier savings.

This problem is inherent in the supposed panacea of privatizing Social Security accounts, which has the financial-services industry licking its chops over the prospect of being able to harvest fees from every employee in America. Even so, allowing workers to invest a few percentage points of their savings into the stock and bond markets might make it possible for them to earn more than the 1.5 percent annual return on their contributions that Social Security currently offers. As it presently stands, the less you contribute to this system, the better an investment it becomes. Unfortunately, when the time comes to cash in, either the price of assets will fall or the cost of what retirees want will rise, until they reach equilibrium.

Remember that the other developed nations in the world (European countries and Japan) have this same problem (an aging population and a skewed demographic) even worse than we do, while the developing ones (China, India, and South America) are net importers of capital, not exporters. We can't look to foreigners to buy all our stocks and bonds. Meanwhile, there will be fewer buyers in the younger generation at home as well. As Gary Lewis and the Playboys asked in the 1960s, "Who wants to buy this diamond ring?" For many, this question may turn out to be prophetic.

Still other theories propose that importing labor into the country (through increased immigration) will solve the problem by providing the extra workers that the economy needs. However, for this to be effective, we would have to take in approximately five times as many foreign workers per year as we do at present—and a much higher multiple if by chance these people want to bring their families with them. Such a shift would obviously change the makeup of America, and if we go this route, it would be a good idea to screen out as many potential terrorists as possible—no small task. Europe will be facing this dilemma as well, only their workers won't be coming from Latin America, but from Islamic countries such as Algeria. Good luck!

Financiers Robert Arnott and Anne Casscells, in considering all of the above, propose that the most likely outcome is that people simply won't be able to afford to retire. In order to retain roughly the same *dependency ratio* for the working population (that is, the number of parents and children that each active worker is required to support) that's existed for the past 20 years, more people will have to work longer, both to add to the support side as well as to subtract from the debit side, by staying off the rolls of retirees who need supporting. This holds true even if every new retiree is handed a check for a million dollars by the government, since all that would happen is tremendous inflation in the mad crush of retirees competing to buy goods and services from the few remaining workers. In other words, there is no *financial* solution to a *demographic* problem for the generation as a whole.

How does this play out? In Arnott's and Casscells's projection, the baby boomers and Gen Xers will see their retirement ages rise from 64 to 72 between the years 2009 and 2035. Of course, there will be many people who are both unable to retire *and* unable to work. Theirs will be an unenviable lot.

Even postponing retirement may not be the solution it seems. When people plan to work longer, they tend to save even less, because they foresee fewer years needing to be self-financed, so it's not clear how much of a net gain there really would be.

What's Going to Happen?

No one knows. With debt of this magnitude, it's pretty clear that the government can't save you. No one has pockets big enough to pick.

Here's what your authors won't be surprised to see in the years ahead:

- **Cutting benefits.** Well, they won't be "cut," exactly, because this word is taboo when talking about Social Security. Let's say that they'll be "modified" according to different schedules, "reprioritized," or "targeted" to help the truly needy. The government will no longer give money to people who don't really need it ("means testing"), and benefits will be taxed at a higher rate. In other words, benefits will be cut to the bone.

- **Delaying benefits** by raising the mandatory retirement age. Maybe not "raising" it, exactly, but changing the payout contingencies so that retiring earlier will be unaffordable, and doing so later will be inevitable.

- **Raising taxes** by escalating payroll and Medicare taxes and raising marginal tax rates. Perhaps a European-style value-added tax (VAT) will join the mix, so the country can run two gigantic tax systems instead of one.

- **Inflation.** This one is too good to pass up: It raises taxes and reduces the debt in one swoop, with no legislator having to take the blame.

However the Social Security and Medicare burdens are allocated, it's not going to be pretty. Perhaps the other two legs of the retirement stool will hold you up?

Leg Two: Benefits from Work

Until fairly recently, most Americans were covered by a defined-benefit pension plan at their place of employment. These promised lifelong benefits after workers retired, and frequently contained an adjustment for the cost of living. They grew tax deferred, unaffected by inflation or shocks from the market, and they were usually tied to a worker's latest (and therefore highest) salary with the company, as well as to total years of service. Furthermore, the pension was there whether or not the employee chose to save, and the underlying investment portfolio was professionally managed, requiring no brain work on the employee's part beyond showing up in the morning and punching the clock. The only downside was that if you left your job before you were vested (as Americans were wont to do), you lost the benefit. A great deal like this was bound to disappear, and it has. The defined-benefit pension plan is becoming deader than disco.

According to the federal Pension Benefit Guaranty Corporation (PBGC), which oversees these programs, some 7,500 such plans have been shut down since 2000 alone. Why? Various reasons have been given, but one that stands out is that they're too expensive for management to offer. Consider the near-bottomless liability for future payouts under this arrangement, and you'll see why.

24

In 1978 the defined-contribution plan was born: the 401(k) and its ilk. This gave workers the option of leaving some of their salary behind (tax deferred, often with a partial employer match) and managing the investments themselves, with results that we'll examine in a moment. Later, when the idea came to hand employees back the cash value of their remaining defined-benefit plans (remembering that the biggest payouts were end loaded, making it cheap to pay off workers early), and then let them worry about what to do with it, management was all over this like polka dots on a bikini. Today, only 16 percent of Americans receive guaranteed-benefits pensions from their employers.

Happiest of all are government employees. Their pensions are backed by the taxing and borrowing power of the government, a formidable line of defense. Many can retire at age 50 with sensational benefits. In fact, the private sector—which couldn't possibly afford such generous benefits itself—ends up having to pay for the government-pension bonanza. If you want to retire comfortably and early, work at the post office.

Employees in the private sector are less fortunate. If you have a corporate defined-benefit pension that's fully funded, feel free to stand up and dance a jig. The problem is, it's difficult to know for sure whether your plan actually *is* fully funded. You can check your company's latest 10-K filing with the Securities and Exchange Commission, where there will be a table listing both the plan's "benefit obligation at year end" and "value of plan assets at year end." Compare these two numbers.

Alternatively, get a copy of your plan's tax Form 5500 from your benefits administrator. Under Schedule B, Item 2A, you'll find the plan's assets, while Item 2b(4) lists the current liabilities (we warned you that this wasn't easy).

Either way, the great hope is that assets equal or exceed liabilities, and that they'll continue to do so in the future. The Bush administration is pushing Congress to require companies to let workers know if their plans are in trouble, and this seems like a good idea.

Although you may have a defined benefit on paper, it's possible that the fund has been mismanaged and is now underfunded for meeting its coming obligations to you. Instead of prudently pairing future liabilities with maturity-matched government bonds, the managers may have bought stock (hoping to turn the workers' pension program into a profit center). Then, possibly, the stock went down, and they now have a problem: There's not enough money in the account to cover the future liabilities.

By a strange quirk of law, U.S. pension accounting allows a company to book income even when the fund experiences losses (because the "income" is based on *expected*, not *actual* returns). In other words, pension assets can be put on the balance sheet without having to record underfunded plans as a corresponding liability. Recently, the government gave a major gift to pension plans by letting them discount their future obligations by using an even higher assumed interest rate looking forward.

All these accounting games do nothing except paper over the problem. Meanwhile, when a pension plan fails, the promised health-insurance benefits usually go out the window along with it. This is no small matter to anyone affected.

Some 30,000 single-company defined-benefit pension plans still exist. If your employer is one of these and falls into bankruptcy, or if the plan becomes seriously distressed, it may be taken over by the above-mentioned quasi-governmental Pension Benefit Guaranty Corporation. Starting from that moment, no more benefits accrue. The maximum that can be paid out is set at $44,386 a year (but watch for that amount to shrink), no matter how much you were supposed to have coming, and highly paid workers who retire early find their benefits cut even more. The PBGC does not insure medical benefits at all.

Last year, United Airlines (UAL), by virtue of filing for bankruptcy, was able to stop paying into its defined-benefit pension plan. UAL has paid $50 million in insurance premiums to the government, and yet, if they bail on their pension obligations, the PBGC will be stuck with a tab of $8 billion—just from this one company.

There are presently a half-dozen firms who have unfunded liabilities that are greater than their entire market capitalization, and if the markets tumble, there will be many more. In 2002, 360 of the businesses in the S&P 500 had plans that were underfunded to the tune of $216 billion. Because companies can manage their own defined-benefit pension plans internally, instead of being forced to hand them over to a third-party insurer, the existence of a taxpayer-funded agency ready to bail them out when times get tough is an ever-present, tempting option. By agreeing to insure private pension plans, but then radically undercharging for this insurance (premiums haven't been raised since 1994), the government has put itself in jeopardy, while providing a massive bailout to financially unsound companies—first the steel industry, then the airlines . . . can the auto industry be far behind? If a number of these plans run aground at the same time that the Social Security and Medicare deficits come due, who knows to what extent workers will be helped? Will the PBGC get the money it needs? There would be a lot of chicks asking for that worm.

Unfortunately, *the United States has no one to pass its financial buck to except the U.S. taxpayer, and taxpayers in aggregate cannot tax themselves into solvency.* Last year, the PBGC had a deficit of $23.3 billion, and it foresees "reasonably possible" pension defaults of $96 billion. We realize that this sounds like a trivial sum when we were just talking about *trillions* of dollars, but it's not peanuts—just ask any of the 518,000 retirees who are currently receiving checks from PBGC instead of from the company pension plan on which they were counting. Overall, PBGC insures some 35 million participants. The pension liability has the potential to mushroom into one of the largest financial crises in U.S. history.

401(k) Plans

The 401(k) plan is the standard retirement vehicle facing most American workers today. These are directed by the workers themselves and contain assets of about $1.9 trillion in total. If you compare this figure with the $72 trillion needed just to keep Social Security and Medicare afloat, you can see right away that this solution is not going to be enough for everyone to retire to the south of France.

While the 401(k) plans have the advantage of being portable from job to job, they have serious drawbacks. One of the first was noticed when the Internet-telecom bubble burst in 2000 and workers found that the rug had been pulled out from under their stock portfolios. Despite the rules laid down by the Employee Retirement Income Security Act of 1974 (ERISA), workers at smaller companies (where most Americans are employed) often have access to only a few poor

27

and expensive investment options. Still other corporations assign the business of managing their 401(k) plans to a vendor with the expectation of favors in return, such as future business relationships. The final mutual funds that appear on the plan's menu may be there not because they're the best available, but rather because the funds simply paid the plan sponsor to be listed, usually by some revenue-sharing arrangement (a fact not disclosed to workers).

Meanwhile, plan participants often assume that the funds are free, because the expenses are conveniently deducted from performance numbers and not broken out as a separate charge. And since the workers (not the companies) are footing the bill, there's little incentive to keep costs down. For example, while you might buy a diversified portfolio of stocks and bonds at Fidelity Investments for 0.1 percent per year, workers in large plans typically pay 1.17 percent per year in expenses, according to a study by HR Investment Consultants. In medium-size companies (about 50 employees), the fees rise to 1.4 percent, on average; and for small companies, they can be as high as 3 percent per year. These seemingly small amounts make an enormous difference to your investment returns over time.

The biggest problem, however, is that employees haven't proven to be expert money managers. Many choose to make no contribution at all to their 401(k) plans, even where there's a matching contribution from their employer. They may be living hand to mouth and need every penny that they earn.

Only 8.4 percent make the maximum allowable contribution, according to the Center for Retirement Research at Boston College; and when they do pay in, they frequently don't know how to manage their investments. Their employers, fearing lawsuits, are extremely loath to get in the business of providing advice on this topic. Somehow, a lunchtime PowerPoint presentation plus a raft of confusing marketing materials and small-typeface prospectuses from the mutual fund "families" don't seem to be turning us into a nation of crackerjack investors.

Where companies offer both defined-benefit pension plans and 401(k)s, the professionally managed defined-benefit plans outperform the worker's choices by about 1.9 percentage points per year, according to a study by the National Center for Policy Analysis. This may not seem like a big deal, but it adds up to an enormous difference over time.

More damning is this study's finding that the 401(k) plans of workers for major financial service firms like Morningstar, Prudential, Citigroup, and Merrill Lynch—people who earn their livelihood giving financial advice to others—underperformed simple market indexes by anywhere from 3.2 to 10.5 percentage points per year (this study covered the years 1995 to 1998, the last period for which data was available at the time it was written in 2001). If even *these* people can't manage their own 401(k)s effectively, what hope is there for everyone else?

Let's look at the kind of investment choices workers are making. The Hewitt 401(k) Index tracks the daily transfer activity of 1.5 million 401(k) plan participants with a total of about $90 billion in collective assets. As of August 2004, Hewitt Associates found that 24 percent of these workers' assets was invested in their own company's stock. This is a terrible choice, since a decline in an employer's fortunes can lead to a layoff at exactly the same time as the 401(k) implodes. Less than half of these workers' 401(k) assets were invested in diversified stocks and bonds, and 27 percent was warehoused in money-market or stable-value funds, virtually guaranteeing an insolvent retirement. The overall allocation is shown in Figure 1.1.

29

Figure 1.1: Workers' 401(k) Asset Allocation 08/2004

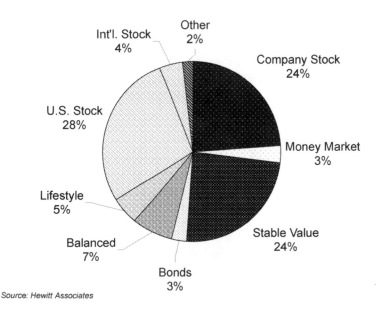

Source: Hewitt Associates

For the coup de grâce, 42 percent of workers simply cash out their 401(k) plans when changing jobs, funneling their retirement savings into current consumption.

In a few years, when these individuals retire and find their piggy banks empty, the Krakatoa of all class-action lawsuits will arrive. The companies that employed them will be put on trial for having failed in their fiduciary responsibility and could be held liable—a black cloud hanging over the stock market and corporate earnings at exactly the point when we'll need a vigorous economy to help shoulder the social burden of the baby-boom and Gen-X retirement. Your authors see the career path of class-action trial lawyer as a growth industry in the future.

The average 401(k) account balance for individuals age 50 to 59, a cohort careening toward retirement, is $88,000. In other words, there's no pot of money sitting in their employee retirement accounts that's going to save them either, which just leaves the third leg of the retirement-funds stool.

Leg Three: Personal Savings

Even if government benefits and corporate pension plans are in jeopardy, perhaps baby boomers have enough in the way of personal savings to see them through their retirements.

According to the U.S. Census bureau's Survey of Income and Program Participation, in 2000 the median net worth of households headed by 55- to 64-year-olds was $112,048; subtract home equity, and that number fell to $32,304. Since then, the housing boom has undoubtedly inflated the value of their homes, although (as many have seen by checking their stock portfolios) what a bubble gives can quickly be taken away. Younger boomers, aged 45 to 54 years, had a median net worth of $83,150, and not counting their homes, their value was $23,525. It may be that the value of these assets will climb a lot between now and when they retire. However, they're off to a slow start: Both the S&P 500 and the Dow Jones Industrial Average were higher in 2000 than they are today.

If this median-net-worth household of 55- to 64-year-olds were to retire tomorrow and somehow manage to get a 10 percent return on their $32,304 (they couldn't do this safely, of course, but imagine that they could), they'd have $3,230.40 a year to supplement whatever they receive from Social Security and their defined-benefit pension plans, if any. This isn't a lot to live on. We hasten to add that, according to AARP, less than 15 percent of boomers expect to receive an inheritance of any magnitude.

Table 1.1 shows the median worth of U.S. households in general in 2000.

Table 1.1: Assets Held by U.S. Households 2000						
Home	Car	Bank Accts.	IRA/ Keogh	401(k)	Mutual Funds	Business Equity
Percent Who Own 66%	85%	64%	21%	27%	27%	11%
Median Value $59,000	$5,875	$4,000	$24,000	$20,000	$19,268	$10,000

Tables 1.2 and 1.3 drill down a bit further, focusing on 45- to 54-year-old and 55- to 64-year-old heads of households, outlining their median financial and nonfinancial assets. This data is from the 2001 Survey of Consumer Finances conducted by the Federal Reserve Board. It includes the 401(k) accounts we mentioned above, but not defined-benefit pension plans (which are difficult to value).

Table 1.2: Financial Assets Held by Baby Boomers

Head of Hshld.	Check. Acct.	CD	Sav. Bonds	Bonds	Stocks	Mutual Funds	Retrmnt. Accts.	Life Ins.
Age 45–54:								
Percent Who Own	92%	15%	21%	3%	22%	20%	63%	31%
Median Amount	$4,600	$12,000	$1,000	$60,000	$15,000	$38,500	$48,000	$11,000
Age 55–64:								
Percent Who Own	94%	14%	14%	6%	27%	21%	59%	36%
Median Amount	$5,500	$19,000	$2,500	$60,000	$37,500	$60,000	$55,000	$10,000

Table 1.3: Nonfinancial Assets Held by Baby Boomers

Head of Hshld.	Vehicles	Residence	Other Property	Other Nonrsdntl. Property	Business Equity	Other
Age 45–54:						
Percent Who Own	91%	76%	15%	10%	17%	7%
Median Amount	$15,700	$135,000	$65,000	$56,400	$102,000	$11,000
Age 55–64:						
Percent Who Own	91%	83%	18%	12%	16%	8%
Median Amount	$15,100	$130,000	$80,000	$78,500	$100,000	$30,000

Of course, lest these paint too rosy a picture, we also need to take into account the debt these folks owe, which is shown in Tables 1.4 and 1.5.

Table 1.4: Debts Held by Baby Boomers

Head of Hshld.	Home Mortgage	Other Residntl.	Instlmnt. Loans	Credit-Card Balances	Lines of Credit	Other
Age 45–54:						
Percent Who Own	60%	7%	46%	50%	2%	7%
Median Amount	$75,000	$33,500	$9,600	$2,300	$5,300	$5,000
Age 55–64:						
Percent Who Own	49%	8%	40%	42%	3%	7%
Median Amount	$55,000	$40,000	$9,000	$1,900	$20,500	$5,000

Table 1.5: Debt of the Boomers

Head of Household	Debt Payment > 40% of Income	Debts Past Due 60 Days
Age 45–54:	9%	6%
Age 55–64:	11%	6%

A glance at these tables will show something missing—namely, anything like the massive amounts of capital that will be required to sustain the baby boomers and Gen Xers through their retirements. The amount of private savings they've accumulated is grossly inadequate.

Figure 1.2, which is from the U.S. Bureau of Economic Analysis, shows the percent of disposable personal income that Americans have been saving lately.

Figure 1.2: U.S. Personal Saving Rate

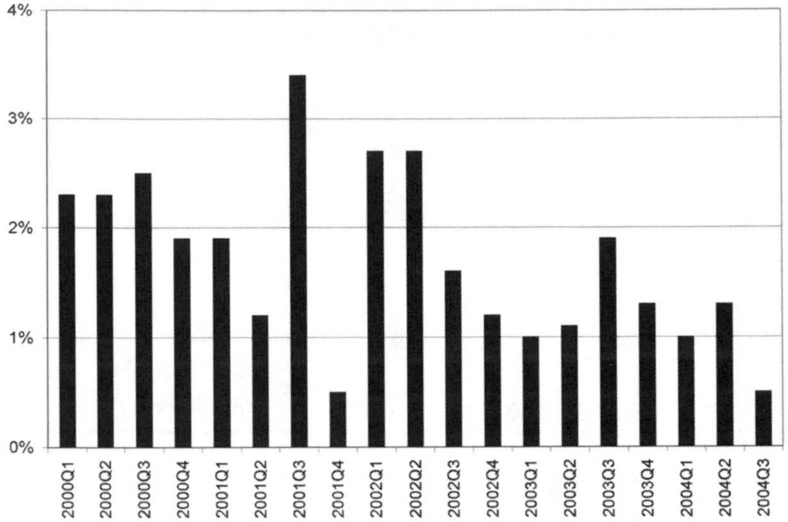

Personal saving accounted for 0.1 percent of disposable personal income in October 2004, down from 0.3 percent in September. These aren't the savings rates of a nation that's aggressively preparing for the future. If the English are a nation of shopkeepers, then Americans are a nation of shoppers. You can't extrapolate from savings rates like these and come anywhere close to where we need to be.

Whether you look to government redistribution programs, corporate pensions, 401(k) plans, or other private savings, it's just not in the cards for 78 million baby boomers to knock off work and play golf for 23 years. Where's all the cash going to come from to support them? It doesn't exist. If the government tries to print the money anyway, it will ruin the currency. If it tries to tax its way out of the mess, the economy will be crushed.

Ten percent of senior citizens already live below the poverty line. This is no way to spend your days when you're old. Your authors fear that many in our generation are going to be joining their numbers.

What's more, the retired baby boomers are going to be living well compared to Gen Xers, because the bones will be picked completely clean by the time they retire.

Having said all of this, we'd like to add one more thing: Yes, you can still retire comfortably. Maybe not everyone will, but *you* can, and we're about to tell you how. Don't get overwhelmed with the fate of the whole generation. Just worry about yourself, and then plan and act. You don't need to outrun the bear; you just need to outrun the other hunter.

Read on.

■ ■ ■

CHAPTER 2

Save Yourself

I f it hasn't sunk in already, the Woodstock generation is about to learn that love isn't all you need. You also need money.

In the 1990s, when the boomers started to turn 50, retirement still felt manageable. Despite the problems with Social Security and the disappearance of the defined-benefit pension plan, two pillars held up their dreams of one day retiring as country-club millionaires. One was the indomitable stock market that swelled their IRAs and 401(k) plans by 20 percent or more each year; and the second was the high interest rates readily available on T-bills, certificates of deposits (CDs), and money-market funds. Once they cashed in their hefty stock portfolios, a handsome rate of return assured that they'd always be flush with plenty of spending money in their pockets.

Then, in March 2000, the stock-market bubble burst, vaporizing $7.7 trillion in paper wealth and forever changing the retirement landscape. The thrill of participation in that joyride cost the boomers more than their savings—it cost them time. Looking back, the switch from the defined-benefit pension plan to the defined-contribution 401(k) plan had proven a disaster.

In an outcome predicted by The Game of Life (a childhood favorite for many), a lucky group will move on to Millionaire Estates and live in swinging resort communities with cocktails, golf tournaments, and the latest designer drugs and replacement organs, while others, less fortunate, endure far more modest lives of privation. This is one of the central dramas that will be unfolding before your eyes over the coming decades. From the outside, two people may look like they have approximately the same lifestyles today—but a time will come when one goes on to a better life and the other moves to the poorhouse (or its modern equivalents).

What is to be done? In 1915, Ernest Shackleton's boat *Endurance* became trapped and finally crushed by Antarctic ice, stranding him and his 27 men many thousands of miles from home without their boat, on an ice floe. They had certain knowledge that no one was coming to rescue them. So, in a shining moment of leadership, Shackleton gathered his freezing crew and announced, "We are our own rescue party."

Twenty-two months later, after an epic struggle of man against nature (even earning a reference in T.S. Eliot's *The Waste Land*), every one of them survived.

We say the same thing to the boomers and Gen Xers: Nobody is coming to save you. No Santa Claus is going to appear. If you want to retire comfortably, you're going to have to save yourself.

You're not going to accomplish this by sitting around complaining, or by worrying, or by living in a fantasy land, but by taking a fearless inventory of your situation. Then you have to prepare.

Save, Save, Save

Unless you are a person of independent means, the importance of a regular program of saving cannot be overstated. The future is coming, and it should be on your mind today. Yet, astonishingly, only 62 percent of baby boomers saved any money in 2001. This is a train wreck in the making.

Your authors know many people who don't save much, but instead focus their energies on finding a brilliant investment scheme that will earn fantastic returns and thereby rescue them. Perhaps they watch CNBC for stock tips, follow some investment guru, or use a "black box" software program or technical analysis, or peruse a newsletter to pick the just the right stocks and funds that will leave the others in the dust. This is a sucker's game. The ones left in the dust are the suckers.

It is vastly more important that you hit upon a pretty good investment allocation (such as the one we'll present later on in this book) and save aggressively, than that you save little but invest brilliantly. The former is the road that leads to Millionaire Estates.

Serious saving runs counter to the practice of most Americans, who, as we've shown, put aside only a tiny sliver of their disposable income, on average. Instead, they like to drop their dollars into current consumption. Watch the ads on TV and you'll notice that the happy people are the ones out shopping and buying. Open a magazine, and it's the same story. All this getting and spending is great for the economy: It drives up corporate earnings and acts like a giant happy pill for the stock market.

In fact, if everyone took our advice and started saving instead of spending, it would be a disaster. It would trigger a severe recession, if not an outright depression. Stores would sit full of goods but empty of customers. More capital would be available to companies for expansion, but to no good purpose, as there would be no consumers to buy what they sell.

We think that the odds of everyone in the country heeding our counsel are nil. Only some individuals will save—a distinct, self-selected minority. Everyone else will go on spending as before: like there's no tomorrow (a self-fulfilling prophecy if ever there was one). If they're reckless enough to buy houses for zero percent down, financed by interest-only, floating-rate loans, they aren't going to let a little thing like preparing for retirement many years away stop them.

The fact that most people can be relied upon to ignore this extremely simple, basic, and obvious advice has important implications. First, it suggests that while there may be a recession or depression in our future, it won't be one caused by excessive saving on the part of the baby boomers and Gen Xers. Second—and this is the important part as far as you're concerned, dear reader—*those who do save will gain a tremendous advantage over those who don't.*

Consider the fact that if everyone were to save equally, then this would confer no net advantage on anyone. We'd all be pitted against each another to exchange the same quantity of stocks and bonds for the same goods and services from younger Generations X, Y, and Z. But if some save and some don't—a state of affairs we deem certain—then the retirees who have assets will be living large when their counterparts who failed to save will find the cupboards bare.

39

Making a few sacrifices today is a small price to pay to avoid being old and destitute later. In fact, we can put it even more starkly: No sacrifice made while you are young or middle-aged is too great if it helps you avoid the worst possible fate—penury in old age.

Please stop for a moment and try the following thought experiment: Picture yourself as a child, and then think about what you might like to do for that child, what you'd like to tell this "little you," if you could go back in time and help him or her. What a difference you might make! Except that . . . you can't. You're powerless to change the past.

Now, visualize yourself as an old person. Imagine that you have the power today to see to it that this older you is comfortably well-off. "You the older" looks at a map and sees a world of places he or she would like to travel. You play golf three times a week if you want. You can walk into a car dealership, a clothing store, or a fancy restaurant with your head held high. You have money to entertain and socialize with friends. You can help your children with the down payment for their house and send your grandchildren to good schools. You have enough to donate to charity, buy meals for the homeless, and support PBS and the local symphony orchestra. In short, you're a person who commands respect, a person with dignity.

Alternatively, you can make this older you poor, sick, and stressed out with worry about money. "You the older" can toss and turn at night figuring out how to pay the MasterCard and Visa bills, and wondering what's going to happen to your spouse if he or she needs to go into a state-run nursing home. It's a lonely, agonizing feeling churning inside: the constant knowledge that you had your chance to prepare and blew it.

When you've got no money, people can see right through you. Even the bus driver treats you with silent contempt. Being poor is like being radioactive. It shouldn't be that way, but that's the way it is. The point of retirement planning is to deal with the world as it is, not with some alternate reality where every story has a happy ending.

Here is something amazing: This is your choice right now, today. It's in your hands. You are deciding which life this "future you" will have. Like a child, this future self is completely dependent on you and the decisions you make today. To *not* make a decision which course you choose is still to make a decision. The future is coming, ready or not. The most important thing you can do today is to decide to save, to take care of yourself. This isn't going to be easy, though, and you need to examine some of the pros and cons.

First of all, it will mean jumping off the treadmill of mass-consumer culture. You'll no longer be deriving your self-worth from the ownership of high-status possessions, or from fantasies of owning those things. In the race to keep up with the Joneses, it means graciously accepting defeat—or at least refusing to play the game. People who lead glamorous, "high-flash" lifestyles today are either so rich as to be completely irrelevant to your life or confused souls who don't see the "Bridge Out" sign ahead.

The decision to save (and thereby to save yourself) means bidding good-bye to conspicuous consumption and competitive acquisition, because these—like a drug—give you a short-term high, but leave you nowhere except feeling vaguely guilty and wanting an escape from this psychological prison . . . which means needing even more. *More* also means more expensive, so in order to get keep getting the same high, you have to increase your spending, and you never catch up—you're forever a rat running in a wheel. This isn't to say that this path leads nowhere. On the contrary, it leads directly to poverty in your old age.

If you're married or in a committed relationship, you'll have to get your partner on board with the program. If your spouse is a compulsive shopper, a fashion victim, or someone who uses spending as an antidepressant, it's not going to do much good for you to be saving all by yourself. And if you aren't married yet, it's a good idea to look at how your prospective mate handles money: "First I look at the purse," as the song goes. Is he or she a big spender? That habit may not be as cute when the money runs out.

Our good friend and legendary investor Jim Rogers tells the story of how when he was first married, his wife wanted to buy an expensive dining-room set. He told her that they could buy the fancy furniture today, or they could invest that money in the stock market and have a lot more cash tomorrow. Jim prevailed, and today he's worth billions.

It's more work psychologically to save today in order to have enough money tomorrow. You have to resist the onslaught of subliminal

41

messages telling you that you're worthless unless you're handing money to someone. After all, it's easy to go to the mall and have teenagers sell you merchandise. It's harder to entertain yourself in a way that doesn't involve opening your wallet.

Apart from the obvious trade-off that doing this gives you a fatter purse to open later (when you need it), it has an immediate payoff as well: It makes you a better person. It builds character. This is what happens when you pay less attention to your image and more attention to your reality. When you live in the real world, you become more real yourself.

There are helpful resources for this lifestyle change all around you. Consider for a moment the humble public-library card: It costs nothing, yet it's a magic carpet taking you to an endless source of entertainment and fulfillment. Instead of spending Saturday afternoon at the mall, you can keep company with the greatest minds who ever lived. When you read *Moby Dick,* you become a deeper person (in spite of what the French deconstructionist critics say). And there's more there than the classics: Take a look at the latest John Grisham offering; a collection of music CDs, audio programs, and a whole college education's worth of audio courses from The Teaching Company that feature more entertaining lecturers than you ever heard in school; there are also DVDs and magazines. If they don't have something, they can probably get it from some larger system of which they're a member. An afternoon spent in your library will enrich you, just as an afternoon of shopping will drain you.

Speaking of reading, there's a vast literature on the subject of saving and staying out of debt. The classic on the subject is Benjamin Franklin's *Poor Richard's Almanack*, which you can read for free on the Web or get from your library (it's no coincidence that Franklin founded the first public library in the United States).

While a wealth of information is available, here are some basics that will help you save:

— **Buy your home.** Unless you have extremely unusual financial circumstances, you'll want to become a home owner. People who own their homes are different from everyone else: They're richer. It's not just that they have more money so they buy property. It's because they're invested in society and save in a way that people who don't have money in the game do not. In 2001, home owners had $175,000 in net worth, compared to under $7,000 for people who didn't own. Home owners had $91,000 in other assets besides their homes, compared to the $7,000 for the rest of the population. Look at Figure 2.1 to see how stark this comparison is (the data is from the AARP Public Policy Institute).

This difference isn't explained away by age or other demographics. Home owners are savers, savers are home owners, and the home is the main saving vehicle for most Americans. In order to become a saver, buy your home.

Figure 2.1: Net Worth of Home owners vs. Non–Home owners in 2001

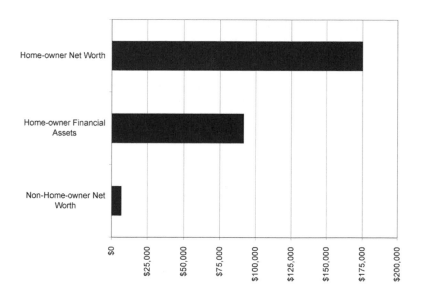

43

— **Get out of credit-card debt.** It goes without saying that you can't begin to plan for retirement if all you're doing is sending in the minimum on your monthly credit-card bills. Unless you pay off your balance in its entirety every month, these cards are destroying your soul. Put down this book and get out of credit-card debt—that's the first job. In fact, there's little justification for almost any kind of consumer debt, with the exception of a home mortgage.

— **Cars:** Americans love to drive, and we're no exception. One of your authors, Ben Stein, just bought a used American car for $28,000, and it's a great vehicle. An auto dealer would have cheerfully sold him a fancier model, or even a vastly more expensive one, but Ben's more concerned about saving for retirement.

We live in Los Angeles, where $80,000 seems to barely get an entry-level vehicle, and so many people drive BMW 745s that it almost looks as if they must be issued at the county line. But in truth, almost no one can afford a vehicle with such a high price tag.

One of your authors recalls leaving an orchestra concert at Severance Hall in Cleveland and watching the Severance family depart after the evening's program. This is a family with enough spare change to donate concert halls for symphony orchestras, so what grand carriage did they climb into? A Toyota Camry. That's the type of car that "old money," rich people drive, and the truth of the matter is that almost no one needs anything pricier than a Mercury Grand Marquis.

You'll also save a fortune if you get out of the habit of leasing a new car every three years. An excellent guide to buying your next ride is on the Motley Fool Website, which will put your head on straight regarding the whole process (**www.fool.com/car/car.htm**).

— **Clothing:** This is another ego-driven area where people compulsively overspend. If anyone needs to wear more expensive clothes than he or she can buy off-the-rack at Brooks Brothers (or, better still, at a Brooks Brothers factory outlet), we've never met him or her.

Here's a little fashion secret that we guarantee will make you look thinner, more beautiful, more interesting, and nearly irresistible to the opposite sex: Have a lot of money in the bank. You'd be amazed what a turn-on having money is.

— **Investing:** Over the years, your authors have made every boneheaded investing mistake in the book, so you don't have to. Ben Stein's humorous book *How to Ruin Your Financial Life* details them all. Shortly, we'll be presenting you with a method for investing that has every chance of minimizing your mistakes in this area. The importance of following a prudent course here can't be overstated, because errors with your investments are among the most costly you can make.

— **Dining out:** When Starbucks sells you a coffee-flavored drink for three dollars, you have to understand that it's not really the coffee you're buying (the coffee is actually quite bitter, which is why people rarely drink it straight)—it's the Starbucks "experience"—that is, getting to feel like a caffeinated yuppie and all the self-worth that goes with it. We recommend that you get your self-esteem somewhere else and save the money.

We don't mean to pick on Starbucks—it's a brilliant company. But if you can get into the habit of eating at home, entertaining at home, and preparing food at home for consumption at work, you'll save a fortune.

One final thought. You may remember a newsletter from a few years back called *The Tightwad Gazette.* It's no longer published, but all thousand-plus pages of it have been assembled into a book (*The Complete Tightwad Gazette* by Amy Dacyczyn), which you can buy used on Amazon for less than $12 or check out from your library for free. Leaf through it and you'll discover countless ways to save money. Best of all, you'll learn the joy of becoming a value-conscious consumer.

Here's another great way to get started: Keep a notebook and write down every purchase you make for a week. This will raise your awareness, as well as immediately suggest a number of relatively painless ways to cut back on your spending.

Maximize Your Human Capital

Human capital refers to the physical, psychological, and intellectual assets you possess that enable you to earn money. It's this that allows Asians who arrive on our shores as "boat people" refugees with nothing more than the shirts on their backs to become millionaires in one generation.

Physical Capital

Your most important physical asset is your health. If you're sick or have a chronic disability, it's harder to earn money than if you're otherwise fit. Just as important, the self-care habits you practice now will prove to be extremely important later in life. You may be 30 years old and in terrific health, but if you smoke, drink to excess, or carry 60 pounds of extra weight, these things will take their toll on you by the time you're old.

At one level, they might kill you prematurely, thus ending the question of your retirement forever. But they might ruin your quality of life and cause you to require expensive, chronic care. If, at age 70, you find that you're unable to afford the bills, you might have to settle for life as a ward of the state. That won't be a fun way to spend the last decades of your life. So please take good care of yourself, whatever your age.

Psychological Capital

Your psychological capital refers to things like your character, resiliency, perseverence, and ability to get along with others. Most people who get laid off aren't fired because they lack the physical stamina or intellectual horsepower to do the job. Often, they're sidelined because they're misfits who don't know how to work well with others, and when the time comes to make cuts, they invariably rise to the top of the list. Having the psychological flexibility to "go along to get along" is an extremely valuable attribute.

It's said that America runs two schools: the academic school system (grades pre-K through graduate school), which is very forgiving and easy; and then work school, which starts afterward, and is tough. If you're a prickly prima donna who lets the least little thing get you bent out of shape, you're going to find the American workplace a very tough school. It will chew you up and spit you out.

Psychological skills, such as the ability to get along with others, are also important in your relationships. If you're married and can stay that way, you'll generally be far richer than if you split up. Divorce may be "no-fault" these days, but it's also tremendously expensive to start your life all over again.

Another important part of your repertoire is cultivating habits of self-discipline and hard work. The boss knows who the hard workers are. People who give their all and who have good attitudes get promoted, while clock-watchers and narcissists get pushed to the margins. That's the way it goes in a meritocracy.

Intellectual Capital

This includes both what you learned in the classroom, as well as the training and special skills you may have picked up along the way. If we have any young readers who are still in school, we urge you to take the hard courses. Don't avoid math and science, and if possible, go to graduate school in an area that pays money to those with the right degree (Icelandic poetry doesn't count—law, business, and medicine do). Hollywood is forever telling us to follow our bliss, but there's also something to be said for having a job.

We mention this especially because one of the most celebrated archetypes in our culture is that of the rebel: the guy or gal who refuses to fit in, breaks all the rules, and only does things his or her way. A smart-ass attitude and a contempt for ordinary working stiffs completes the picture. The problem is, even though these sorts of heroes do well in movies, in real life they tend to be losers—especially when they've passed their 15th birthday. Despite the sneers it gets from Hollywood and Ivy-League intellectuals (who always seem to think that they know better than the rest of us), the middle-class American way of life is paradise on earth and the envy of the entire world.

It may be especially good to gain skills that you might be able to use until late in life, and/or ones that you might practice on a part-time basis, but this isn't as easy as it sounds. No one knows what the careers of tomorrow will be, nor what will be outsourced. If you're currently being paid $35 per hour to assemble transistor radios, it's very likely that your job will be handed over to someone in China who will be happy to do it for a much lower fee. On the other hand, jobs that have a high-touch interface and can't be outsourced (such as bricklayers or massage

47

therapists) may be positions that you don't quite feel physically up to in your 70s or 80s. Nursing is another prime example: There will undoubtedly be a high demand for nurses as the population ages, but unless you're in administration, it can be physically demanding work that's better suited to the young.

One positive aspect to this demographic trend is that there's likely to be a shortage of people to fill the available jobs. Older people who are otherwise willing and able to work should be able to find employment. While anyone who can stand up might get a job as a Wal-Mart greeter, the hope is that you could acquire specialized skills that earn a higher wage—perhaps consulting in your previous field of work or developing a second career in an area that's not physically strenuous and can't be done conveniently via the Internet from Bombay. There's a whole literature on the subject of careers for seniors that you could consult for ideas in order to see where your interests intersect. If you can find a second employment path that's with the government, so much the better: Any benefits will be gilt-edged, and—unlike almost everywhere else in the economy—they won't discriminate against you on the basis of your age.

The reason we stress human capital is not only because it can help you earn more money and therefore add to your savings. Just as important is this: *After you retire, any money you can replace through part-time employment is money that you won't have to draw from your savings.* To say nothing of the fact that work greatly adds to your self-esteem and, in Freud's words, binds you to reality. The best kind of income stream you can have (apart from a large one) is one that's diversified. If you can still earn money late in life, you'll be better off than if you have to depend entirely on the vagaries of the capital markets.

Postpone Retirement

You've probably read that the original retirement age of 65 was set by Chancellor Bismark back in the 19th century, but this is wrong—Germany's initial retirement age was 70. Mandatory retirement at 65 goes back to the U.S. railroad pension system in 1874, when it was considered the maximum age at which a worker might safely drive a train.

Later, the federal Railroad Retirement Act of 1934 institutionalized this arrangement, which served as the template for President Roosevelt's committee when Social Security was established in 1935.

Today, nearly three-quarters of working Americans opt to retire at age 62—coincidentally, the earliest age that Social Security benefits become available (the latest data show men retiring at 61.6 and women at 60.8 years), but postponing solves a multitude of problems in a single step.

First, the longer you delay taking your Social Security benefits, the more money you can receive each month. A person who earns $40,000 a year theoretically receives an inflation-adjusted $834 per month by retiring at age 62, but if she waits until she's 66, she receives $1,140—and if she can hold out until she's 70, she pockets $1,572 a month. Taking Social Security early is an advantage if you're going to die before age 76; but if you're going to live to be older than 81, waiting works to your advantage. It can also be of tremendous benefit to your surviving spouse, so don't leave that factor out of the hopper.

Unfortunately, the legislative risk attendant upon the revision of Social Security could throw off these contingencies, making this case less than ironclad. One of the first things the government is expected to do is raise the age at which these benefits kick in, which will make the decision to retire later even easier.

A second reason postponing retirement works to your benefit is that it gives you a longer period of time to add to your nest egg, and for the savings that you've accumulated to compound. Every year counts, especially toward the end, when there's a larger base amount upon which to earn interest. The more you have saved up, the better for your retirement.

The third reason, less happy to contemplate, is that for every year you continue working, there's one less year for your savings to support you.

Unlike in the 1930s, most of today's sexagenarians aren't worn-out from a lifetime of hard labor in the mines or the fields. In most cases, there's no physical necessity whatever to retire. If you have a job, you always have the option to quit if it becomes intolerable. If you aren't employed, you may never have the option of getting your old position back again, and you may have to settle for less—possibly a lot less. Think of Albert Brooks in *Lost in America,* quitting his lucrative career as creative director at a major advertising agency in Los Angeles, only to have to take a job as a school crossing guard after his money runs out (because his wife lost it in Las Vegas).

Saving, maximizing your human capital, and working longer are the basic ways to secure your retirement. In the next chapter, we're going to focus on saving.

■ ■ ■

PART II

HOW MUCH TO SAVE AND HOW MUCH TO SPEND

Having outlined the dimensions of the retirement-funding crisis and sketched the path to a solution—for you, if not for everyone—the next few chapters are going to walk you through how much money you need to save starting today, how much income you'll need after you retire, and how to grow a nest egg to provide this amount. We're going to tell you exactly how to invest your money so that you have the greatest likelihood of meeting your goals. Finally, we're going to outline how to draw down your accounts once you've retired, to squeeze every penny from them that you can—safely.

CHAPTER 3

How Much Will You Need?

For the Bill Gates and Warren Buffett types among our readers, here's an easy way to plan your retirement: Put 50 times your annual income into inflation-indexed bonds. The 2 percent interest that they pay will effectively re-create your salary throughout your retirement while keeping up with inflation. These bonds are an extremely secure investment, backed by the full faith and credit of the United States. If you follow this strategy, when you go to the happy hunting ground, your heirs will get your fortune intact (well, after paying the death taxes).

What's that—you don't have 50 times your present salary to invest? Okay, here's another way to do it: On the day that you retire, take your salary, multiply it by the maximum length of your retirement (say, 35 years), and put that amount in T-bills. They're extremely safe, and the interest they pay tends to keep up with inflation. Then every year, for the rest of your life, withdraw your salary (adjusted for inflation). Your heirs will receive whatever's left over (although if you live to your maximum life span, you'll die broke and they'll get nothing).

There's just one problem with this second scenario: Where are you going to get 35 times your current salary? *Barron's* editor Tom Donlan got it right (as usual) when he wrote: "If [Americans] ever figured the cost of 35 years of retirement protected against inflation, they would drop dead now and save themselves a lot of worry."

Alas, in these short paragraphs, we've already exhausted all of the easy, risk-free approaches to retirement. The rest of this chapter is for everyone else.

How much will you really need to have in savings when you retire? Like all long-range questions with many intervening variables, this is extremely difficult to answer with precision. However, the inherent indeterminacy doesn't mean that you should sweep it under the rug, pour a martini, and forget about it. Even a glance at the numbers will sound a Klaxon warning to most of you: You need to save more—a lot more—than you reckoned on, and you need to start immediately.

How much you'll require is really a two-part question: How much income will you be replacing from your personal savings after you retire, and how long will you need it for?

How Much Income Will You Need to Replace?

The general advice about how much money you'll need to live on after you retire (compared with how much you're living on now) varies widely. We've seen estimates ranging everywhere from 15 percent of your pre-retirement income (for those wishing to live in the park, foraging for nuts and berries?) to 120 percent. This is far too broad a spread to be of any use, so let's look at what goes into making these guesses.

Perhaps the biggest difference between pre- and post-retirement is that you'll no longer necessarily be salting away a significant portion of your income year after year into IRAs, Keoghs, 401(k)s, and other accounts. If you've been saving 15 or 20 percent (or more) of your income annually, this laborious process will come to an end and the difference will go straight to your bottom line.

In addition, your average tax rate might fall after you retire. At the very least, you'll no longer be having payroll taxes deducted. However, the income from your tax-deferred savings accounts (except for Roth IRAs) will be taxed as ordinary income as it's withdrawn—even if it consists mostly of reinvested dividends and capital gains—and who knows how high future tax rates will be? Over the course of the 20th century, they ranged from zero to more than 90 percent, so even if you could predict your future investment returns to three decimal places, the unknown rate at which you may be taxed would be enough to make you throw up your pencil in despair.

Meanwhile, any savings that you kept in taxable accounts may (or may not) have a close shave coming in the form of capital gains taxes when sales are made. This will hold especially true if you started saving early. At present, the long-term capital gains tax rate is 15 percent. What adds insult to injury is that most of this amounts to a tax on inflation: The poorer a job the government has done in maintaining a stable currency, the more taxes you have to pay. For example, if you bought a stock in 1950 for $10 and sold it in 2000 for $20, that actually represented a capital gains *loss* after inflation, but it wouldn't have stopped the IRS from taxing you on the nominal profit anyway.

Unfortunately, we don't know what the capital gains tax will be when you retire—it's ranged from zero to 49.875 percent over the past century. Also, don't forget that your state tax board might want to give your profits a haircut as well.

If you want to play with some numbers that *might* anticipate how you'll be affected, go online to **http://taxes.yahoo.com**. It's quite possible that your effective tax rate might fall by five or ten percentage points—but it's also possible that it won't. Taxation is the wild joker in the retirement deck.

The bitter truth is this: *Those of you who have saved for retirement are likely going to be made to pay for those who haven't, through some process of governmental confiscation of your wealth.* After Uncle Sam takes his bite, you'll also have friends and relatives in need desperately knocking at your door, some of whom you'd probably like to help. Remember that episode of *The Twilight Zone* where a dinner party is interrupted by an air-raid siren, and the family who had the foresight to build a fallout shelter finds their friendly neighbors battering down its door in order to get away from the impending nuclear holocaust? It's going to be like that.

Does this mean that you should just forget about saving? Not at all. Those on government assistance will be living lives of real misery (reread *The Grapes of Wrath* for a preview). You need to save even more so that you don't become one of them.

If you've arranged to pay off your home by the time you retire, so much the better. There may be cases where the value of some other investment exceeds the benefits of eliminating your mortgage, but probably not many. It also must be said that a long-term mortgage is a significant inflation hedge and has a tax advantage for those who item-ize and aren't otherwise snared by the alternative minimum tax. But being free of this monthly burden will do a lot to lighten your financial (and psychological) load. This payment is money that you won't need to replace (although the taxes, insurance, and home repairs that make up the "pride-of-ownership" experience will continue until the end of time, so they need to be in your budget).

Much celebrated is the newly minted retiree's ability to shed need-less work-related expenses. If you have the kind of job where you're forever lunching at the Four Seasons on your own dime, wearing cus-tom-made English suits and commuting by personal helicopter, these expenses can really add up. Most of the time, however, it just means that you'll no longer be buying bus tokens or getting your shoes shined as often. Unless you plan to get rid of your car or retire to a nudist colony, you're still going to be driving and wearing clothes. We suspect that for most people, these work-related savings might add up to a couple of percentage points a year.

Against all this, there are going to be plenty of *increased* expenses after you retire. If you hadn't noticed, health care is a sector of the American economy where prices haven't exactly been going down lately, and retirees are this industry's biggest customers. Need glasses, a hearing aid, or a crown on your molar? Sorry, you're not covered. If you've been working for a corporation with typical gold-plated health benefits, you're suddenly going to be paying for Medicare premiums and Medigap insurance out of your own pocket. These policies aren't cheap, and they're getting more expensive all the time. So, too, are long-term-care policies, should you wish to insure against the prospect of a protracted stay in a nursing home or other assisted-living situation. These expenses will undoubtedly exceed whatever rate of inflation the government is posting.

On the more positive side, leisure travel, recreation, entertain-ing, and new hobbies can also be expensive. As Dr. Seuss says, oh, the places you'll go! Like, to the poorhouse if you're not careful. You may have a new car now, and maybe couples can get by with one car instead of two, but at some point you're going to have to replace it. In fact, you'll probably be buying several new cars before you drive off into the sunset, so you'd better plan for this in your budget. And—

prepare to be very afraid—what happens when you get that phone call from your daughter at 3 A.M. telling you that she's just left her husband and has the kids in the back of the minivan . . . and she needs your financial help to make a new life?

So How Much, Already?

Expectations rise throughout our lives. When you were 16 and working an after-school McJob, the prospect of a studio apartment with cable TV and a mattress on the floor sounded like the Playboy Mansion. Fifty years later, this setup doesn't have the same appeal.

In 2001, the median income for Americans ages 45 to 54 was $41,104; it was $35,673 for those 55 to 64; and it was $19,688 for individuals 65 and older. In others words, people over 65 were living on 48 percent of what their cohorts a decade younger were earning. This suggests that people experience a declining income as they move past midlife, and indeed, that's the sober reality. Yet in our experience, everyone much prefers to maintain or improve their standard of living. They don't mind having more money to spend, but dislike having to tighten their belts.

As people age, they're either losing interest in worldly things (entering what Hindus call the *sannyasa* stage of life, wandering the roads as spiritual ascetics with begging bowls), or alternatively, they're making due with less and not loving it. Our guess is that the 10 percent of retirees living below the poverty line are not loving it. Here's our conclusion:

- It's safe to assume that you are going to wish that you had 100 percent of your pre-retirement income after you stop working. Four out of ten current retirees say that their income needs today are equal to what they were pre-retirement, according to the Employee Benefit Research Institute, so you should fall to your knees in thankful prayer if you can match your pre-retirement income.

- That said, most people will be extremely lucky to re-create even 80 percent of their previous paychecks.

57

This 80 percent figure is the target you frequently hear from financial planners. The problem is that it's based on studies of individuals over their entire retirement, and it makes no provision for the fact that young retirees a-go-go want to spend more. Young retirees are in a second adolescence—one without parents breathing down their necks—and they require plenty of folding green to keep them in golf shoes and convertibles. Middle retirees tend to slow down, so they don't spend as much. But then, late in the game, health spending looms large, so provision must be made for that as well.

Your authors don't use the 80 percent mark because we feel that it's optimal for retirees, but we didn't just pick it out of a hat, either. We chose it because we think that it may be attainable for the kind of thoughtful baby boomers and Gen Xers who have been concerned about their retirements, planning, and saving—those who are likely readers of this book. The 80 percent solution will probably keep you in something similar to your current lifestyle without necessitating the more dramatic accommodations that a lesser target might require. It's not far out of line with results found by the 2004 Georgia State University Retiree Income Replacement Project, which are summarized in Table 3.1. These figures show the percentage of previous income needed in retirement to equilibrate the lifestyle of a 65-year-old wage earner and a 63-year-old nonearning spouse.

| Table 3.1: Replacement Income Needed After Retirement | |
Final Salary	Post-Retirement Replacement Percentage
$30,000	84%
$40,000	81%
$50,000	79%
$60,000	79%
$70,000	80%
$80,000	81%
$90,000	82%

Whither Social Security?

Social Security, with its built-in cost-of-living adjustments, would be a wonderful platform upon which to build your retirement income, and 66 percent of people 65 and older rely on it for at least half their income. There are those who say that the program is funded through 2038. The early baby boomers will benefit the most, while Gen Xers may be left with little. Long before 2038, however, the payments likely will be "means-tested" (given only to those whose income falls below some specified threshold), so if you're in an above-average tax bracket, you may not get anything.

To find out more about what you might receive, go to **www.ssa.gov**, or read that statement they mail you every year before your birthday. It's best regarded, however, as a work of science fiction—a description of one possible future reality. Read the cover letter that the Social Security Administration includes with it, and you'll see that we're not kidding. As we go to press, President Bush intends to fix the system, and we wish him every success. If you're rich enough to afford this book, you'll undoubtedly be one of those who finds their Social Security check shrinking over time for one reason or another.

The inescapable conclusion for the middle class is this: *You're going to be paying for the bulk of your retirement out of your own private life savings.* As an initial rule of thumb, this means that you'll probably need private savings of 12 to 16 times your final salary, depending on how aggressively you're planning to draw them down and how long a retirement you're contemplating. We'll fine-tune this multiplier for you in a moment, but this shows why the X-factor of an unknown Social Security benefit is so unsettling for middle-class savers.

The lower class will be protected, at least at some subsistence level. In fact, we bring terrific news for those of you living on welfare (assuming that you have no upwardly mobile aspirations): There's little need for you to save at all, because you'll probably be able to continue receiving government handouts forever.

We also bring glad tidings to those of you who are already rich: The loss of even 100 percent of your anticipated Social Security income will make no difference to you, since it was never more to you than money with which to light your cigars and tip the doorman.

For everyone else, though, the news is bad. A family (not an individual) earning a median $45,000 per year will find that it makes an extraordinary difference whether Social Security will be providing the maximum $27,000 in annual disbursements—meaning that the family will only have to generate an additional $18,000 each year from other sources—or if they'll need to cough up the entire $45,000 themselves. This median family might need savings of somewhere between $360,000 and $900,000 to make up what Social Security isn't paying, and it's impossible to predict where along this continuum the answer will lie. We can venture some educated guesses.

If you're retiring today, you'll probably get most of what you expected from Social Security, and it will only taper off gradually, perhaps starting around 2015 or so. If you're retiring in 2025, however, it might be better to assume that you'll get half this dollar amount after your benefits are both cut and taxed; but if your collection date is later and you're a higher-income type (say, someone who earns $80,000 per year or more), you might not see any Social Security benefits at all. (Let us emphasize that these are guesses.)

Even if you predicted the amount of your future Social Security paycheck correctly, it would be nothing short of miraculous if you simultaneously guessed your post-retirement tax rate. Right now, the average Americans of our example might be paying $6,000 to $7,000 in federal income tax, but what if the government decides it really needs $10,000 instead (in order to pay for everybody else who—oops!—forgot to save)? This puts the average retiring couple on the path to a very different future, and throws their savings plan into a cocked hat. If you're in the middle part of the middle class, having to revise your budget a few thousand dollars below what you were expecting might be extremely difficult, because there's not much elbow room.

The moral of all this is that *you have to err on the side of oversaving.* You need to keep every penny that you can, because the uncertainly of the future means that you need to be more prepared, not less. This isn't just your authors' crank doomsday scenario: It's the mainstream, consensus view of the researchers who have examined the topic. The main exception is the Congressional Budget Office, which thinks that everyone will do just fine. Of course, they only looked at median retirees, assumed they will pay no taxes; Social Security and Medicare won't be cut; and that people won't care if they die broke, leaving their children nothing.

Which brings us to another terrible truth: *The hardest hit of all (in terms of a lifestyle that rolls off a cliff like a BMW X5) will be the upper-middle class.* Are you perhaps a doctor or lawyer, or some yuppie professional? Do you possibly earn several hundred thou a year? If so, you're about to go on a bummer the likes of which you haven't experienced since you took that bad acid at the Fillmore West during the Grateful Dead concert back in '67: First, means-testing will ensure that you never collect a dime from Social Security. Then you're going to be taxed within an inch of your life to pay for everyone else. Why will they pick on you? Because you're where the money is. Because they can.

Now that we've discussed how much income you'll need to replace each year, we're going to take a look at the second factor you need to consider: time.

How Long Will Your Retirement Last?

61

This stage of your life will last from the day that you stop working until the day you die. If you know when you're leaving your job, then you should be able to use a mortality table to predict your life expectancy, and calculate how long your retirement will last by simple arithmetic. All you have to do is get the numbers and do the subtraction, right?

Wrong. With advances in medicine and biotechnology, there's no telling what might happen to life expectancy. In fact, it nearly doubled over the past century as medicine conquered most of the infectious diseases that had people dying young. Today, the big killers are degenerative disorders such as cancer and heart disease—yet a staggering amount of research is dedicated to curing them, and a breakthrough with either one could substantially impact your life expectancy. This may not happen for another century—or it may be as close as tomorrow's headlines. Even without a big discovery, the incremental progress adds up, as you can see by the fact that longevity is increasing over time. Thanks to insurance actuaries, the present rate of escalation is already programmed into the prediction tables, so it doesn't need to be calculated separately and added on to your age.

Also, do you happen to be married? We ask because the predicted longevity of a couple is not simply the same as that of both individuals considered separately. It's longer—at least for the surviving partner.

Of course, the average mortality of someone your age may not apply to you. There's a chance that you might live 10 or 20 years longer. In other words, *you can't plan for the average life expectancy—you have to plan for your maximum life expectancy.*

What's more, *your maximum life expectancy increases over time.* With each year that passes, more and more of your peers die off, leaving you in that elite corps of survivors whose odds of living still longer are enhanced by your having made it this far. A quarter of the people who turn 65 are going to live past 90. The maximum life-span estimate is a moving target that increases at the rate of one bonus year for every decade you survive.

This is a good news/bad news scenario. The positive aspect is that you might live an extremely long life. The negative side is that you're going to have to pay for it.

Where can you find maximum-life-span tables, not just average ones? Right here: Table 3.2 shows how long a retirement you might have to plan for if you're single—how long 5 percent and one percent of people your age live, respectively. Our Website **(www.stein-demuth. com)** will link you to maximum-life calculators for couples, where you can enter both your ages and see how long the oldest member might live. You don't want to look down from heaven and watch your surviving spouse pounding the pavement looking for work when he or she is 100 years old.

Table 3.2: Life Expectancy		
Your Age Today	There's a 5% Chance You'll Live To:	There's a 1% Chance You'll Live To:
40	100	105
45	100	105
50	100	105
55	100	105
60	100	105
65	100	105
70	101	105
75	101	106
80	102	106
85	102	106
90	104	107
95	106	109
100	108	110

As a simplifying rule of thumb, we're just going to assume that there's a 5 percent chance that you'll live to be 100, and a one percent chance that you'll survive to 105. Remember that even at the one percent confidence level, one out of 100 readers might live longer—enough to make them wish they'd saved even more. Don't worry too much about this, though—you'll probably die much sooner.

The main control that you may have over the number of years that your retirement will last (short of a phone call to Dr. Kevorkian) is retiring as late as possible. Not to get into any heavy math, but let's say that your retirement will last for n years. You don't know what the ultimate number will be, but you do know that for every year that you continue to work and postpone retiring, it's $n - 1$.

Now some people argue that life itself is so risky that it makes no sense to try to nail down your retirement at a 99 percent confidence level. For example, there's the risk of nuclear war, a global depression, a giant comet hitting the earth, a vast plague, or some environmental catastrophe—whatever gurgles up from the cauldron of worst-case scenarios. Students of history know that these kinds of bad events are far more the norm than the peace and prosperity that contemporary Americans take as their birthright, and if any of these were to happen, even the best-laid retirement plans might disintegrate. But that doesn't mean you should take up smoking and hang out at French cafés drinking absinthe. At least you can take control of what you can.

Your "Back-of-the-Envelope" Answer

In the next chapter, we'll go into some detail in order to help you figure out how much you need to save, but for those readers who want to cut to the chase without having to do a lot of calculations, we'll present a shortcut. It's so simple that you can jot it down on whatever scrap paper you happen to have handy.

The answers shown in Table 3.3 (page 66) should fit many people's circumstances. All you have to know is your age (look on your driver's license); your salary (look at your paycheck); and how much you have in dedicated retirement savings (look at your brokerage statements), here expressed as a multiple of your current salary.

Go down the column on the left that lists existing retirement savings, and then across the row to the column closest to your current age. Where these intersect, that's the percentage of your gross salary that you need to save, starting today, in order to fund your retirement. (If you're browsing in a bookstore, this table would be a good page to tear out and stick in your pocket when the clerk isn't looking.)

Note especially the assumptions that we've made, which are shown at the bottom of the table. Perhaps the most controversial is that we're assuming you won't get any Social Security. This may be true for younger readers, who at least might be able to count their private Social Security savings accounts as part of their regular savings (if President Bush is successful). But readers close to retirement might get most or all of the benefits that they've been counting on. The higher your income and the further out your retirement date is, the less you can probably expect from the Social Security trust fund. If you do want to factor it in, use the alternative method that we'll describe in the next chapter.

The savings we refer to here must be earmarked specifically for retirement. If you're saving up to buy a house, that's well and good, but it isn't the same thing. These are funds that you must be planning not to touch until you retire. Please be realistic about this. You'll also need to keep several months' worth of living expenses untouched in a money-market fund as a backup system for your life—in case of emergency, break glass. These are also not part of your retirement savings.

If you were hoping to retire at age 65 instead of 70 (as Table 3.3 on page 66 assumes), you can simply add five years to your present age and use the savings rate listed in that column.

Table 3.3: Recommended Savings Rates as % of Current Salary
Conservative Assumptions, Back-of-Envelope Method

Savings	Age 25	Age 30	Age 35	Age 40	Age 45	Age 50	Age 55
I Have No Savings Earmarked for Retirement	8%	10%	13%	19%	27%	41%	66%
Savings = 1/4 of Salary	6%	9%	12%	18%	26%	40%	65%
Savings = 1/2 of Salary	5%	8%	11%	17%	25%	39%	64%
Savings = 1 Year's Salary	3%	6%	9%	15%	23%	36%	61%
Savings = 2 Years' Salary	0%	1%	5%	10%	19%	32%	56%
Savings = 3 Years' Salary	0%	0%	1%	6%	14%	27%	51%
Savings = 4 Years' Salary	0%	0%	0%	2%	10%	23%	46%
Savings = 5 Years' Salary	0%	0%	0%	0%	6%	18%	40%
Savings = 6 Years' Salary	0%	0%	0%	0%	0%	14%	35%
Savings = 7 Years' Salary	0%	0%	0%	0%	0%	9%	30%
Savings = 8 Years' Salary	0%	0%	0%	0%	0%	5%	25%
Savings = 9 Years' Salary	0%	0%	0%	0%	0%	0%	19%
Savings = 10 Years' Salary	0%	0%	0%	0%	0%	0%	14%
Savings = 11 Years' Salary	0%	0%	0%	0%	0%	0%	9%
Savings = 12 Years' Salary	0%	0%	0%	0%	0%	0%	4%
Savings = 13 Years' Salary	0%	0%	0%	0%	0%	0%	0%

Assumptions: "Couch Potato" Portfolio • 1% fees on investments • Live on 80% of final salary after retirement • Retire at 70
No pension • No Social Security • Low (40 percentile) investment returns until retirement • You might live to age 105 (1% possibility).• Your portfolio in retirement has a
1% risk of failure. • Normal Career Path

Table 3.3 makes fairly conservative assumptions, but for those of you wanting to take on more risk by saving less, we present some additional recommended savings rates in Table 3.4. Here we're being more liberal in three specific ways:

1. We're assuming that you'll get a median investment return going forward, not a return at the 40th percentile of what investment returns have been historically.

2. We're projecting your maximum longevity with a 5 percent chance of your living longer than we predict (in Table 3.3 it was 1 percent).

3. We're drawing down this portfolio once you hit retirement at a rate where 5 percent of tested portfolios failed over the span of your maximum retirement (in Table 3.3 it was 1 percent).

Table 3.4: Recommended Savings Rates as % of Current Gross Salary
Moderate Assumptions, Back-of-Envelope Method

Savings	Age 25	Age 30	Age 35	Age 40	Age 45	Age 50	Age 55
I Have No Savings Earmarked for Retirement	6%	7%	10%	14%	20%	31%	50%
Savings = 1/4 of Salary	4%	6%	9%	13%	19%	30%	49%
Savings = 1/2 of Salary	3%	5%	8%	12%	18%	28%	48%
Savings = 1 Year's Salary	1%	3%	6%	10%	16%	26%	45%
Savings = 2 Years' Salary	0%	0%	1%	5%	11%	21%	40%
Savings = 3 Years' Salary	0%	0%	0%	1%	7%	17%	34%
Savings = 4 Years' Salary	0%	0%	0%	0%	3%	12%	29%
Savings = 5 Years' Salary	0%	0%	0%	0%	0%	7%	23%
Savings = 6 Years' Salary	0%	0%	0%	0%	0%	3%	18%
Savings = 7 Years' Salary	0%	0%	0%	0%	0%	0%	13%
Savings = 8 Years' Salary	0%	0%	0%	0%	0%	0%	7%
Savings = 9 Years' Salary	0%	0%	0%	0%	0%	0%	2%
Savings = 10 Years' Salary	0%	0%	0%	0%	0%	0%	0%

Assumptions: "Couch Potato" Portfolio • 1% fees on investments • Live on 80% of final salary after retirement • Retire at 70
• No pension • No Social Security • Median returns • You might live to age 100 (5% possibility). • Your portfolio in retirement has a 5% risk of failure. •
Normal Career Path

What Next?

Once you start saving, you'll continue to dun your gross paycheck for the same initial percentage year after year (not the same *dollar amount*, but the same *percentage* of the total), even though your salary presumably will be rising over time—with inflation, if not due to advancement. You should invest your money according to the principles that we describe in the next chapter.

The big lesson of Tables 3.3 and 3.4 is that the earlier you begin saving, the lower a percentage of your salary that you need to save. For example, in Table 3.3, if you start saving when you're 25, salting away 8 percent of your salary should continue to work for you even when you're 45. But if you wait until you reach 45 to begin, then you'll have to drop 27 percent into your retirement accounts that year—and every year thereafter.

This makes a big difference later in life. If you're 45 but started saving when you were 25, you should still be able to get away with shunting 8 percent of your salary into your retirement accounts. This leaves 92 percent for candy bars and magazines, as well as anything else you feel like buying in middle age. But if you wait until you're 45 to begin and haven't saved anything, you can only consume 73 percent of your salary (and don't forget, you still have to pay taxes). You'll have a lot less disposable income over the next 25 years, while the early savers will be extremely well paid for their self-discipline.

Like everything else, the habit of saving is best acquired when you're young, because *procrastination is extremely expensive.* Time passes linearly, but the extra effort required by starting later rises geometrically, since you've missed letting the magical power of compound interest do the work for you. By starting young, you can get the stock and bond markets to do all the heavy lifting, instead of having to do it all yourself through the brute force of stringent saving. Here's our simple rule for the new millennium: *If you're old enough to have sex, you're old enough to save for retirement.*

Reality-Testing Your Progress

No matter what your recommended savings rate is, you should periodically monitor your progress to see whether you're on track. Every five years, you need to check your work against Table 3.5, which shows how much we think you should have saved in dedicated retirement accounts by different ages, if you used Table 3.3 to set your strategy. Multiply your current salary by the figure next to your age, and that's the amount you ideally should have bankrolled for retirement. If your figures are wildly different than ours (that is, less), you might want to reconsider your program and decide to start saving more.

Table 3.5: Are Your Retirement Savings on Track? Conservative Assumptions Multiple of Current Salary You Should Have in Savings	
Age	**Retirement Savings**
25	0.1
30	0.5
35	1
40	1.6
45	2.6
50	4
55	6
60	8.5
65	12.5
70	16

Assumptions: *"Couch Potato" Portfolio • Live on 80% of final salary after retirement • Retire at 70 • No pension • No Social Security • Low (40 percentile) investment returns until retirement • You might live to age 105 (1% possibility). • Your portfolio in retirement has a 1% risk of failure.*

Table 3.6 shows what we think you should have in the way of dedicated retirement savings if you're following the more permissive approach laid out in Table 3.4.

Table 3.6: Are Your Retirement Savings on Track?
Moderate Assumptions
Multiple of Current Salary You Should Have in Savings

Age	Retirement Savings
25	0.05
30	0.3
35	0.7
40	1.2
45	2.0
50	3.0
55	4.5
60	7
65	10
70	13

Assumptions: *"Couch Potato" Portfolio • Live on 80% of final salary after retirement • Retire at 70 • No pension • No Social Security • Median investment returns until retirement • You might live to age 100 (5% possibility). • Your portfolio in retirement has a 5% risk of failure.*

71

If you're comfortable with these assumptions and answers, you can skip the next chapter and go on to the following one, which discusses how to invest for retirement. But if you'd like to explore a more detailed savings method, one in which you have the flexibility to change some of the assumptions we've made above, read on. For example, if you expect a regular paycheck from Social Security, you should definitely pursue the method we present in Chapter 4.

■ ■ ■

Your Custom-Tailored Savings Plan

With all the factors that go into determining how much you should save for retirement—the amount of income you'll need to replace, Social Security, defined-pension benefits, and the length of your retirement—you might be wary of accepting a generic, "one size fits all" solution. We completely understand. In this chapter we'll guide you through six simple steps that will create a savings plan specifically for your situation.

First, let's look more closely at some of the elements of the puzzle.

Do You Have a "Normal" Career Path or an Atypical One?

A "normal" career path, for our purposes, is one where the final salary you earn might be roughly twice your beginning salary (not counting inflation). For example, if a starting widget maker earns $15/hour and a master widget maker earns $30/hour, this is what we're calling a normal career. And if a starting psychiatrist earns $100/hour and a senior psychiatrist earns $200/hour, this is also normal. What matters isn't the dollar amount, but the difference between where junior workers start and where senior-level workers end up.

Mind you, we mean the typical people who follow the career path—we're not talking about the ones like Dr. Phil who go on TV and earn millions, or the ones who get canned and end up sleeping on a park bench and earning nothing. To save yourself a lot of soul-searching, realize that for our purposes, most people work in what we call normal careers.

If you're on some kind of atypical path, these tables aren't for you. This would be the case if a law associate makes $100,000 in the early years after law school, but a senior partner in the same firm makes $500,000—we'd call this an aggressive career path. If a starting Wall Street analyst earns $150,000 with her Wharton M.B.A., and tends to peak 35 years later at $750,000, this is another atypically aggressive career.

These paths are very expensive, because a large nest egg will be needed to keep you in the lifestyle to which you'll eventually become accustomed. When you work backward to figure out the savings needed in the early days of your working life in order to float this lavish retirement, it's quite expensive as a percentage of your (relatively low) initial salary, even with the benefit of compound interest. The folks in these positions may be getting stock options or other perks later in their careers that make up for it, though. If you're on an aggressive career track, get thee to a financial planner—preferably sooner rather than later. As an illustration of the need for this type of planning, your authors have a friend who earns $700,000 per year, which isn't bad—except that he spends $800,000 annually and he has no savings. At this rate, it's going to be difficult for him to retire.

Do You Think That Investment Returns Will Stay Close to Their Historical Averages or Be Significantly Lower?

The "median" savings rates specified in the tables that follow (pages 82–85) are the 50th percentile returns that our recommended portfolio has earned historically. But if investment returns going forward turn out to be significantly lower than average, you'll need to save even more to make up the difference. The percentage of your salary that you need to put away in order to compensate for the possibility of 25th percentile returns is shown in the next column. These are the numbers to use for those of you who believe that a low-return environment is what lies ahead. Alternatively, you might want to pick some percentage between the two. That's what we did earlier, in Table 3.3 (page 66): To give people a margin of safety, we assumed that investment returns going forward would come in at the 40th percentile. But here we offer you a choice between median returns (50th percentile), and low ones (25th percentile).

Which should you choose? Let's pause for a moment to consider one of the paradoxes of retirement investing. This means contemplating two competing truths, both of which are relevant:

Truth 1: The longer the time frame stretching forward, the more likely it is that your investment results will gravitate toward their historical averages.

Look at Figure 4.1, which plots the maximum and minimum returns you could have received by holding the S&P 500 stock index over varying lengths of time from 1802 to 1997 (data courtesy of Jeremy Siegel's *Stocks for the Long Run*). If you held the stocks for only a year, you might have made as much as 67 percent or lost as much as 39 percent. Wow.

Figure 4.1: Range of Stock Market Returns by Holding Period

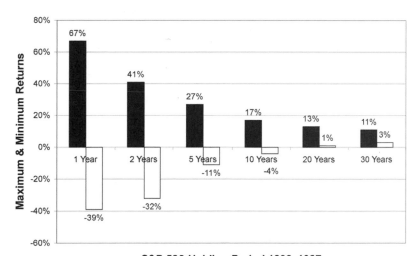

S&P 500 Holding Period 1802–1997

■ Maximum Returns ☐ Minimum Returns

But look at what happens when you hold stocks for a longer period: The range of possible returns shrinks dramatically. Indeed, there was no 17-year holding period where stocks lost money during this time.

So if you're under 45, you're still light years away from retirement—no problem, right?

Wrong. *This data is commonly misinterpreted and misused by retirement planners to make the extremely convenient but completely unwarranted assumption that long-term investors will get average long-term rates of return.* Yes, they might get these returns on average, but not necessarily in particular cases (such as yours). This is because:

Truth 2: The longer the time frame stretching forward, the more likely it is that any particular set of investment returns may wander far, far away from its historical average.

Figure 4.2 shows the results of 1,000 possible future 30-year scenarios with $1,000 invested in the S&P 500, all with the same average returns and variability of returns that were shown to illustrate Truth 1.

Figure 4.2: Range of Possible $1,000 S&P 500 Returns over 30 Years

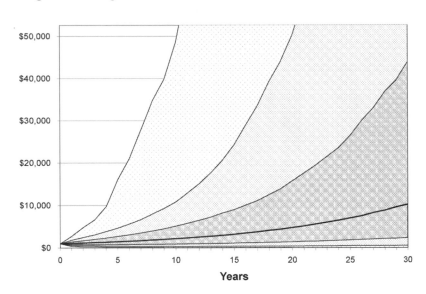

The final values of these accounts range from a high of $1,046,469 to a low of $268, with the median figure clocking in at $10,252. This is an enormous variation. Even the most average among us don't get exactly median returns every year—some years are better, some worse.

The cumulative effect of the particular sequence your returns follow can lead your portfolio wildly askew from what you might expect. This is the "random-walk" effect. The problem is that you don't know which way your investments will veer, so you might end up with far more—or much less—money than you expect.

The point of this hypothetical situation is that *you can't settle the issue once and for all. You have to monitor your performance periodically to see whether your savings are on track* (see Table 3.5 or 3.6, pages 70–71), and make adjustments accordingly. For a greater likelihood that your account will be fully funded, you can increase your rate of saving.

Six Steps to Create Your Savings Plan

To create your custom-tailored savings plan, follow these six steps:

1. Factor in Post-Retirement Expenses. Let's start by figuring out how big a nest egg you'll need. Here's the math:

> Your Final Salary
> x .80 (estimated amount needed after retirement)
> _____
> Your Post-Retirement Income

We're assuming that you can get by comfortably on 80 percent of your pre-retirement income. If you're over 45, it would be a very good idea to use Intuit's Quicken or Microsoft's Money software for a year to get a better handle on your expenses on a line-by-line basis, in order to double-check that this number works for you.

Of course, no one knows what future tax rates will be, which means that there will be a substantial X-factor in your calculations. If you're pulling money from tax-deferred accounts, your withdrawals generally will be taxed as ordinary income; if you're using taxable accounts, you'll have to pay some capital gains taxes.

This 80 percent estimate probably works the best for people in the middle classes. If you earn $10 million each year, cutting back 20 percent ($2 million) might make no practical difference to your lifestyle whatsoever. On the other hand, if you earn $20,000 annually, cutting back 20 percent ($4,000) would hurt a lot. In short, we recommend 80 percent as an average figure, but you can use whatever percentage works for you.

2. Factor in Social Security. Next, you need to subtract your estimated Social Security paycheck from this figure:

> Your Estimated Post-Retirement Income
> – Your Projected Social Security Income
> _____
> Your Adjusted Post-Retirement Income

You can find out how much Social Security proposes to pay you by going to **www.ssa.gov** or by reading that letter they send you before your birthday every year. Then you have to decide: Is this true? Perhaps taking less than the full amount of this figure would be prudent.

3. Factor in Your Pension. Next, subtract your projected annual benefit from your defined-benefit pension plan, if any:

> Your Adjusted Post-Retirement Income
> – Your Predicted Annual Pension Income
> _____
> Your Annual Self-Generated Retirement Income

If your pension benefit is fully funded and has a built-in cost-of-living adjustment, then subtract the full amount. If it doesn't, then you might want to subtract only about half of it. This is because under average rates of inflation, the real spending power of your pension might be cut in half over the course of your retirement. There's also the unpleasant possibility that your plan may run aground at some point.

Once you've done the math, you'll have a fix on how much income you're going to have to replace each year from your personal savings.

4. Calculate Your Nest Egg. The size of the nest egg you'll need depends on three factors:

1.   How old you're going to be when you retire
2.   How much risk of running out of money you're willing to accept
3.   How long you'll live

We've plotted for four different retirement ages: 60, 65, 70, and 75. Retiring later means that you need less money.

In terms of investment risk, we've forecast the probabilities that your portfolio will allow a certain rate of withdrawal and still have you solvent in the end. These are mapped at a 100 percent, 99 percent, and 95 percent probabilities.

We really don't know the 100 percent outside age you might live to. The *Guinness World Records* book cites 122 years as the age reached by the world's oldest human. In the Bible, Methuselah lived to be 969 (Genesis 5:27). We do know that the odds are about one percent that you'll live to 105 and 5 percent that you'll live to be 100, so we've mapped these probabilities as well.

Table 4.1: How Big a Nest Egg Do You Need? Average Returns Multiply Times Desired Annual Retirement Income from Nest Egg:			
Income Safety:	100%	99%	95%
Longevity Safety:	99%	99%	95%
Retire at 60	32.3	21.3	17.9
Retire at 65	31.3	21.3	16.9
Retire at 70	31.3	20.0	16.1
Retire at 75	28.6	18.9	15.2

Assumptions: 0.20% Account Fees After Retiring • "Couch Potato" Portfolio

To use Table 4.1, first look at the left-hand column and pick the age at which you propose to retire. Then, going across the table, you have a menu of choices, depending on how much risk you want to assume in drawing down your nest egg after you retire. The first column represents the lowest degree of risk: a portfolio where no case out of 10,000 ran out of money over your projected life span, and only one case out of 100 had you living longer than the portfolio anticipates. These multipliers are all quite high. Securing this margin of safety with your retirement accounts requires a lot of money.

If you want to keep the same longevity risk (a one percent chance of living longer than this), but are also willing to accept a theoretical risk of one percent that your portfolio might run out of money before you retire (that is, 100 out of 10,000 portfolios went bust at some point during the planned retirement period), move over to the second column. The multiplier drops considerably, meaning that you'll need significantly less savings to fund this option.

The final column raises both your longevity as well as your investment risk to the 5 percent level: You have a 5 percent chance of living longer than the age this portfolio plans for, and your portfolio has a 5 percent chance of going bust before your retirement is through. Taking on these increased risks makes for a smaller multiplier, resulting in the need for less savings today.

There's no magic to these numbers (although they are distilled from millions of calculations). They simply represent the amount of money you'd need in your nest egg to generate your required annual income (which you calculated in Step 1), when invested in our recommended portfolio—the subject of the next chapter.

One interesting feature of Table 4.1 is that it attempts to quantify the trade-offs involved in making these choices. It shows how being willing to take slightly more investment risk makes a much bigger difference to the overall amount of savings required than postponing retirement does. If you opt for the most conservative choice, you'll need vastly more savings than if you're willing to take a small gamble on the risk of running out of money. This is worth considering. Remember that you always have the option of cutting back on your spending before your money runs out, so this eventuality should never occur (we'll have more to say about this later). Cutting back might not be pleasant, but neither would it be catastrophic.

Having picked the multiplier that corresponds to your comfort level, multiply this by the desired annual self-generated retirement income that you calculated earlier, and you'll see how big a nest egg you'll have to supply from your personal savings:

Your Annual Self-Generated Retirement Income
x Multiplier from Table 3.6

_____

Your Required Nest Egg

Don't faint. Keep reading.

5. Calculate Your Annual Savings Amount. Armed with this information, you can calculate how much you need to save each year. This time you aren't going to calculate it as a percentage of your salary, as in the last chapter, but as a fraction of the final nest egg you'll need.

The tables that follow (pages 82–85) are organized by the number of years you are from retirement. Pick the table that corresponds to the time you have remaining in the world of work, and then use that particular one, ignoring all the others.

Once you have determined which table applies to you, calculate the percentage of your final nest egg that you already have sewn up in dedicated retirement savings. For example, if you need a million dollars on the day you retire and you presently have $100,000 in savings, that's 10 percent; $200,000 in savings is 20 percent, and so on. Again, this assumes that these savings are dedicated exclusively to your retirement and that you're going to be investing them according to our specific recommendations. Just go down the left-hand column of the table that matches your time until retirement until you find the "Savings as Percentage of Nest Egg" that most closely matches your own.

Finally, go across to either the "Median" or "25th Percentile" columns. These refer to the assumption you want to make about investment returns from the stock and bond markets going forward. If you choose "Median" returns, you're saying that the historical rates these markets have returned are what you expect to see in the future; while if you select "25th Percentile," you're betting that these returns are going to be significantly lower in the future. The more conservative choice means that your savings won't grow as fast, so you'll need a higher savings rate between now and then in order to generate the same nest egg years hence.

Table 4.2: Percentage of Nest Egg to Save Annually for People Starting 35 Years from Retirement

Future Investment Returns:	Median	25%ile
Savings as % of Nest Egg:		
0%	0.6%	0.8%
5%	0.2%	0.5%
10%	0.0%	0.1%
20%	0.0%	0.0%

Table 4.3: Percentage of Nest Egg to Save Annually for People Starting 30 Years from Retirement

Future Investment Returns:	Median	25%ile
Savings as % of Nest Egg:		
0%	0.9%	1.1%
5%	0.5%	0.8%
10%	0.1%	0.5%
15%	0.0%	0.1%
20%	0.0%	0.0%

Table 4.4: Percentage of Nest Egg to Save Annually for People Starting 25 Years from Retirement

Future Investment Returns:	Median	25%ile
Savings as % of Nest Egg:		
0%	1.4%	1.7%
5%	1.0%	1.3%
10%	0.5%	1.0%
15%	0.1%	0.6%
20%	0.0%	0.2%
25%	0.0%	0.0%

Table 4.5: Percentage of Nest Egg to Save Annually for People Starting 20 Years from Retirement

Future Investment Returns:	Median	25%ile
Savings as % of Nest Egg:		
0%	2.1%	2.5%
5%	1.7%	2.1%
10%	1.3%	1.7%
15%	0.8%	1.3%
20%	0.4%	0.9%
25%	0.0%	0.5%
30%	0.0%	0.1%
35%	0.0%	0.0%

Table 4.6: Percentage of Nest Egg to Save Annually for People Starting 15 Years from Retirement

Future Investment Returns:	Median	25%ile
Savings as % of Nest Egg:		
0%	3.4%	4.1%
5%	2.9%	3.6%
10%	2.4%	3.1%
15%	1.9%	2.7%
20%	1.4%	2.2%
25%	0.9%	1.7%
30%	0.4%	1.3%
35%	0.0%	0.8%
40%	0.0%	0.4%
45%	0.0%	0.0%

Table 4.7: Percentage of Nest Egg to Save Annually for People Starting 10 Years from Retirement

Future Investment Returns:	Median	25%ile
Savings as % of Nest Egg:		
0%	6.2%	7.0%
5%	5.6%	6.4%
10%	4.9%	5.8%
15%	4.3%	5.3%
20%	3.7%	4.7%
25%	3.0%	4.1%
30%	2.4%	3.5%
35%	1.8%	2.9%
40%	1.2%	2.3%
45%	0.5%	1.8%
50%	0.0%	1.2%
55%	0.0%	0.6%
60%	0.0%	0.0%

Table 4.8: Percentage of Nest Egg to Save Annually for People Starting 5 Years from Retirement		
Future Investment Returns:	Median	25%ile
Savings as % of Nest Egg:		
0%	13.8%	15.0%
5%	12.8%	14.1%
10%	11.8%	13.1%
15%	10.8%	12.2%
20%	9.9%	11.3%
25%	8.9%	10.3%
30%	7.9%	9.4%
35%	6.9%	8.5%
40%	5.9%	7.5%
45%	4.9%	6.6%
50%	3.9%	5.7%
55%	3.0%	4.7%
60%	2.0%	3.8%
65%	1.0%	2.9%
70%	0.0%	1.9%
75%	0.0%	1.0%
80%	0.0%	0.1%
85%	0.0%	0.0%

85

6. Adjust for Taxes and Inflation. We're assuming that these monies are being kept in a tax-deferred account (such as a 401(k), IRA, or Keogh), where they'll compound untaxed. If this isn't the case, you'll have to pay taxes on any dividends, coupons, and capital gains from these investments out of separate funds. Otherwise, a regular IRS haircut will ensure that your nest egg never grows as required.

Every year you'll also have to adjust your savings by the rate of inflation. If you save $10,000 in year one and the rate of inflation is 3 percent for those 12 months, you'll have to save $10,300 beginning the next annual cycle, and so on for every year after that. This will keep you even in terms of your purchasing power.

In order to make this process clearer, we're now going to review all six of these steps using a specific example. As you read the sample scenario, keep in mind that retirement planning isn't about having exact numbers or trying to nail everything down to three decimal places. None of us can foretell the future to anything remotely like that degree. Instead, it's about making trying to make broad, intelligent estimates.

An Illustration of This Method

Let's consider a couple in which both individuals are 51 years old with a median income (for their age) of $58,045; they're planning to retire in 15 years, when they hit age 66. From Table 3.2 (page 63), this suggests that it might be wise for them to plan for the possibility of a 35-year retirement.

86

1. Adjust for Post-Retirement Income Requirements. We're going to assume that 80 percent of this couple's pre-retirement income will be enough for them to get by:

$58,045 (Annual Income Today)
x   80% (Estimated Percentage
            Needed After Retirement)
_____

$46,436 (Required Post-Retirement Income)

2. Adjust for Social Security. If both partners work and each earns half of the household's annual income, Social Security proposes to pay them $24,312 a year (in today's dollars) when they hit 66. However, we're going to bet that it won't all be there when they want it. Let's assume that by the time they go to collect, they'll only get 75 percent:

$24,312 (Social Security Promised Annual Income)

x   75% (Discount Factor)

$18,234 (Realistic Social Security Estimate)

So we're looking to Social Security to provide a floor to their income of $18,234. Obviously, the assumption made here has an enormous impact on everything else. We're trying to make a reasonable guess—somewhere between the Panglossian projections put out by the government and the Cassandra warnings of the doomsayers.

We can now calculate how much income they'll need to replace every year out of their nest egg by subtracting what Social Security might provide from their total annual need:

$46,436 (Desired Post-Retirement Income)

– $18,234 (Social Security Income)

$28,202 (Adjusted Post-Retirement Income)

3. Adjust for Defined-Benefit Pension Plan. Like most Americans, our median couple doesn't have a defined-benefit plan in place to help pay for retirement, so this step is easy:

$28,202 (Adjusted Post-Retirement Income)

– $0 (Predicted Annual Pension Income)

$28,202 (Annual Self-Generated Retirement Income)

Our median couple still needs to generate $28,202 from their nest egg annually.

4. Calculate the Total Nest Egg Required. In order to do this, we'll get the magic multiplier from Table 4.1 (page 79). Looking down the barrel of a 35-year retirement and shooting for 99 percent probability of portfolio survival with 99 percent longevity survival, we find the multiplier of 21.3. This number is derived from the assumed real rate of return that savings might grow over the next 15 years, if invested according to our guidelines in the next chapter. We multiply it by the amount of income this couple will need to replace each year in order to arrive at their required nest egg.

$28,202 (Annual Self-Generated Retirement Income)

x   21.3 (Multiplier from Table 4.1)

$600,702 (Nest Egg)

In other words, it looks as if they'll need a nest egg of $600,702 on the day they retire in order to generate the necessary annual income from their personal savings. (We've accounted for the effects of inflation in all of these calculations.)

5. Calculate How Much More to Save. Since we're looking at a median-boomer couple, let's say that they have the median financial assets of $56,000 (2001 data), or roughly 10 percent of their final nest egg . . . okay, 9.3 percent, but who's counting? We're making estimates here, not launching the space shuttle.

Since they're 15 years from retirement, we'll turn to Table 4.6 (page 83), go down the left-hand column to the 10 percent savings figure, move across to the median-returns column, and voilà: 2.4 percent. This suggests that they should save 2.4 percent of the final-nest-egg value each year between now and the day they retire, assuming that they achieve average investment returns between now and then.

$600,702 (Nest Egg)

x   2.4% (Percentage from Table 4.6)

$14,417 (Annual Savings Required
to Build Nest Egg)

They need to save at least $14,417 annually for the next 15 years in order for their retirement to be fully funded. This is 25 percent of their gross annual income, and even this is based on getting median investment returns until they retire, so you can see why the median family needs to get saving right away.

This figure also assumes that they start putting money away right now. If they wait another five years, they'll have to use a different multiplier that will be much more unfriendly—the amount more than doubles!

6. Adjust the Annual Savings for Inflation and Taxes. Finally, they have to adjust the amount they save every year by the rate of inflation. What's that figure? We'll link to it from our Website **(www. stein-demuth.com)** so that you can make this calculation for your own situation. If inflation is 3 percent during the first year, then for the second year, our median couple needs to save 3 percent more:

$14,417 (Initial Savings Rate)

x   3% (Inflation Rate Year One)

_____

$433 (Additional Savings Needed Starting Year Two)

89

. . . which means: $14,417 + $433 = $14,850 . . . and so on for each successive year, adding to the amount from the prior 12 months (or subtracting, in the unlikely case of deflation).

This step is necessary to keep them even in terms of purchasing power. Presumably, their income is rising along with inflation, allowing them to make this further contribution to their retirement accounts without additional pain.

There's just one more hitch: As we mentioned earlier, we're assuming that these dollars are being kept in tax-deferred accounts so that the sums can compound unmolested by the IRS. If they have to keep them in taxable accounts, then it's essential to pay any dividend and capital-gains taxes that they generate out of separate funds—not out of the retirement account itself.

To make this entire process a little easier for you, we've put together a worksheet where you can enter your own figures.

Retirement Savings Worksheet

Step One: Adjust for Post-Retirement Income Needs

1. Your pre-retirement income _____

2. Estimated % needed after retirement (default = 80%) _____

3. Desired post-retirement income _____

Step Two: Adjust for Social Security

4. Realistic annual social security income estimate _____

5. Subtract Line 4 from Line 3: _____

Step Three: Adjust for Defined-Benefit Pension

6. Realistic annual pension income estimate _____

7. Subtract Line 6 from Line 5: _____

Step Four: Calculate Nest Egg

8. Get multiplier from Table 4.1. _____

9. Multiply Line 7 times Line 8 to get nest egg needed. _____

Step Five: Calculate Necessary Savings

10. Current retirement savings _____

11: Divide Line 9 by Line 10. _____

12. Get multiplier from Tables 4.2–4.8. _____

13. Multiply Line 12 times Line 9 to get annual savings. _____

Step Six: Adjust Savings Annually

18. Increase savings by rate of inflation. _____

19. Pay taxes separately if savings are held taxable accounts.

Further Reflections

The assistance of a fee-based financial planner (preferably one with a Certified Financial Planner designation) can bring a finer point to the analysis, assuming that you can find one who has expertise in retirement planning. Don't assume that because your stock broker or insurance agent blithely refers to him- or herself as a "financial planner" that they have any such expertise. You need to get your advice from someone who doesn't have a stake in selling you high-margin, commissioned products.

With such huge sums needed so far in the future, and with the nature of compound returns from investing being so variable from year to year, it can be difficult to judge whether you're on course. At the very least, it's essential to check your progress periodically. We can think of worse New Year's resolutions than to review your retirement finances before the Rose Bowl every year.

If you're a couple, and inconveniently enough, don't plan to retire on the same day or year, the firepower of a financial planner becomes even more germane. At a minimum, however, you can each calculate your own rates based on your individual savings, expenditures, and investments (even if you commingle them in practice). Then you can look over each other's shoulders at your respective timetables to see if and when the shoe will pinch.

There's an obvious trade-off here between present consumption and future penury. If the investment gods smile upon you, your savings will grow and you'll be blessed with an abundance of riches to draw upon later. In the event that you then find your retirement coffers overflowing, you may kick yourself for having excessively robbed your present lifestyle from being all that it could have been. The problem is that you won't know which course your investments will follow until you get there.

You could be planning to retire next year with your savings on track, but then this year turns out to be a stock-market disaster and your total portfolio is worth 25 percent less by retirement day. The alternative future reality, where you spend too much today and run out of money when you're old, is too horrible to contemplate.

All of this means that you have to err on the side of excessive savings now—you're better off being wrong this way than risking being old and poor. If you've put away 150 percent of what you need to retire, and you're fully confident that this amount will be enough, then—and only then—should you consider cutting back on your savings.

If you have a solvent defined-benefit pension plan, expect to get steady income from Social Security, stand to receive a large inheritance—or are lucky enough to be married to someone who fits one of these descriptions—you're in a far better position than the person who has to self-pay his or her own way for everything. If you don't find yourself on any of these paths to saving for retirement, it's worth taking virtually any measures short of robbing a bank to get on them. No one is coming to save you. You have to save yourself.

Next we'll consider how to best invest your savings for retirement. . . .

■ ■ ■

CHAPTER 5

Investing for Retirement

Most people's investment portfolios are a mess: a hodgepodge of whatever products brokerage houses were pushing in the past, a fistful of overlapping mutual funds, huge bets on their employer's stock, and some hot tips du jour from TV pundits (and don't forget the inevitable sediment of tech stocks at the bottom that were never sold because that would be tantamount to admitting that buying them was a knuckleheaded mistake in the first place). The portfolios that your authors see are almost invariably textbook examples of amateur investing mistakes 101—even portfolios held by those who are otherwise extremely smart and who have a lot of money. As a result of these poor choices, almost everyone was seriously hurt by the pricking of the stock-market bubble from 2000 to 2002.

What you want is some easy way to get out of the gully, to make it as if that whole nightmare never happened. That is wishful thinking. The truth is that no stock-market elixir can make the damage go away. Anything you do now to turbocharge your returns will involve desperate risks of the kind that you couldn't afford to take back in 1999, the kind that got you into this predicament in the first place. This brings us to another important point about retirement: *Don't even think about investing superaggressively to make up for lost time.* Extra rewards invariably entail additional risks, and if the markets turn against you, you could be wiped out. This isn't the time for all-or-nothing thinking.

Although no one wants to hear it, the answer now is the same as it was before that bubble: an extremely diversified, low-expense, tax-efficient, indexed, transparent portfolio that seeks nothing more (but also nothing less) than to glean the market rate of return from the money you put at risk in the capital markets. It's not flashy, it won't wow your friends, and it doesn't make for stimulating conversation at the watercooler or on the putting green. It is, however, the smart move. The rest of the answer is to stick with it and not be swayed by any idiot friends or self-serving advisors who claim that they want to help, but really just want to get you down in the same hole that they're in.

So, how *should* you invest for retirement?

Short Answer: The Couch Potato Portfolio

Financial columnist Scott Burns christened the "couch potato" portfolio. It consists of two investments: the total stock market index and the total bond market index, as shown in Figure 5.1.

Figure 5.1: The Couch Potato Portfolio

Total Bond Market
50%

Total Stock Market
50%

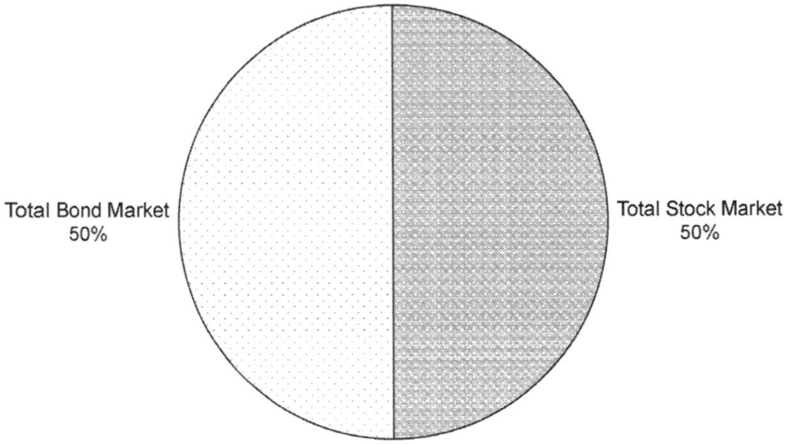

These indexes instantly, cheaply, and efficiently diversify your holdings across the entire U.S. stock and bond markets, in exactly the same proportion as exists in the national economy. Since capitalism is inherently a profitable system, this approach requires no special stock picking, fortune-telling, or short-term market timing to make money.

The positive long-term returns from the stock and bond markets are lying there on the table for anyone to take.

On the stock side, most of the total stock market index mutual funds are based on either the Dow Jones Wilshire 5000 Index or the Russell 3000 Index. The Wilshire 5000 measures the performance of all U.S.-headquartered stocks (although today it includes more than 5,000 companies), weighted according to their market capitalization. The Russell 3000 is a similar index that samples about 98 percent of this same group. By owning these funds, you'll have an infinitesimal share of thousands of companies and participate in their growth and the revenue stream that they generate from operations.

On the bond side, the Lehman Brothers' Aggregate Index tracks the debt instruments of Lehman Brothers' U.S. Government/Corporate Bond Index, Mortgage-Backed Securities Index, and Asset-Backed Securities Index. It includes all the publicly traded investment-quality debt in the United States that has at least one year until maturity and an outstanding par value of over $100 million.

You want to own bonds because the money that you lend to the government, its agencies, and U.S. corporations is invested by them in ways that they believe will add value to their enterprises, and so they're willing to pay you a market rate of interest for the loan of your capital. In practice, at least over the past century in the United States, bonds have been less volatile than stocks (with commensurately lower returns). Investors who owned both stocks and bonds achieved a better rate of return for the level of risk that they assumed than people who had either just stocks or bonds alone. This diversification is extremely important to building your portfolio smoothly over time. Just ask anyone who was invested 100 percent in NASDAQ technology stocks in 2000.

Most efforts to add value through stock picking, fortune-telling, or short-term market timing actually subtract from the returns that are readily available through indexing. These methods require expertise that is expensive to acquire, yet surprisingly, rarely adds value. Trying to beat the market is analogous to trying to beat a $20 quartz Timex by purchasing an expensive gold Rolex with a jeweled, Swiss-made, automatic movement: Buying the latter may make you feel like a big shot, but it won't tell time as accurately, in spite of its high price.

With the couch potato portfolio, your investments are in a two-horse race, and you own both horses: the entire U.S. stock and bond markets. As the wisdom of adopting a simple indexed approach has percolated into investors' consciousness, more and more opportunities have emerged to create this type of portfolio—even in many otherwise terrible 401(k) offerings. This approach is simple and doable for most individuals. If President Bush is successful in allowing workers to divert a portion of their Social Security contributions into private savings accounts, these choices are both likely to be options on the menu, and you should take advantage of them.

Some of the major index funds tracking the total U.S. stock and bond markets are listed in Table 5.1 for your shopping pleasure.

Table 5.1: The Couch Potato Portfolio

Total Stock Market Index Funds

Fund	Ticker	Expense
Fidelity Spartan Total Stock Market Index	FSTMX	0.10
Vanguard Total Stock Market Index Viper	VTI	0.15
Vanguard Total Stock Market Index	VTSMX	0.20
iShares Russell 3000 Index	IWV	0.20
TIAA-CREF Equity Index	TCEIX	0.26
T. Rowe Price Total Equity Market Index	POMIX	0.40
Schwab Total Stock Market Index	SWTIX	0.53

Total Bond Market Index Funds

Fund	Ticker	Expense
Dreyfus Bond Market Index	DBIRX	0.15
iShares Lehman Aggregate	AGG	0.20
Vanguard Total Bond Market Index	VBMFX	0.22
Fidelity U.S. Bond Index	FBIDX	0.32
Schwab Total Bond Market Index	SWLBX	0.43

There's no need to own more than one from each category (that is, one total stock market fund and one total bond market fund), since their long-term performances should be quite similar in each group. We ranked them in descending order of fees because these charges subtract directly from returns. The lower the expenses, the better.

Several of the investments listed (the ones with three-letter tickers: VTI, IWV, AGG) are closed-end funds, which must be bought for a commission from a broker. For long-term savers, the other open-end funds work better, because they reinvest dividends and capital gains by default, letting your savings compound seamlessly.

If you run out of room in your tax-deferred account, you might want to put the remainder of your bond portfolio into an intermediate-term, low-expense, national-municipal-bond fund. Vanguard has one (ticker: VWITX) that may be to your liking. But don't bet the farm on municipal bonds—if Congress ever gets backed up against a wall, it may threaten to repeal their tax exemption, and their value could plummet.

The couch potato portfolio is the foundation of all of the calculations in this book. We've run tens of thousands of simulations assuming the historical rates of return from these asset classes and the variations of these returns, as well as taking into account their correlation. We've used this information as the basis for making all our predictions about how much you need to save and how much you can withdraw after you retire. If you choose not to use this portfolio, there's certainly a possibility that your returns will surpass ours. But we believe that there's an even larger chance that they'll fall short—even significantly short—of the benchmarks we've set. If you decide to go in some other direction, then you're on your own.

97

This isn't to say that the couch potato portfolio is the greatest choice in the world, and it's perfectly possible that you can design a better one. But if you do, please be sure that you know what you're doing, and in what specific way you expect to see improvement. In fact, we'll save you the trouble and suggest a small revision of our own. . . .

Improvement:
The "Thinking Man's" Couch Potato Portfolio

This version has tweaks that might improve the performance of the couch potato portfolio. We have a couple of concerns that the original couch potato strategy doesn't address:

1. **Inflation:** We've seen that a bout of inflation will go a long way toward solving the government's debt problem, albeit at the expense of investors—especially retirees living on fixed incomes. So we have no problem if you want to put half of your bond portfolio in inflation-indexed bonds. We've listed some mutual funds that specialize in these in Table 5.2. For tax reasons, it's best to hold these in tax-deferred accounts.

Table 5.2: Inflation-Indexed Bond Funds

Fund	Ticker	Expense
Vanguard Inflation-Protected Securities	VIPSX	0.18%
iShares Inflation Protected Securities	TIP	0.20%
TIAA-CREF Inflation-Linked Bond	TCILX	0.30%
American Century Inflation Bond	ACITX	0.50%
Fidelity Inflation Protected Securities	FINPX	0.50%
T Rowe Price Inflation-Protected	PRIPX	0.50%

2. **Currency Devaluation:** With America so dependent on foreign investment, many experts believe that our currency, the beloved U.S. dollar, is in decline. This could affect the prices of many of the things you buy, which are increasingly made in other nations (either in whole or in part). For this reason, we have no objection to moving half of your stock portfolio abroad. More than half of the global economy is located outside our country, so this merely indexes your equity holdings to the world (rather than the domestic) stock market.

Once again, we're going to recommend an index-based approach: the Morgan Stanley Europe, Australia, and Far East (EAFE) Index. This is a free-float-adjusted market-capitalization index designed to track market equity performance of developed countries, excluding the U.S. and Canada. The nations it tracks include Australia, Austria, Belgium, Denmark, Finland, France, Germany, Greece, Hong Kong, Ireland, Italy, Japan, the Netherlands, New Zealand, Norway, Portugal, Singapore, Spain, Sweden, Switzerland, and the United Kingdom. Table 5.3

lists some funds that follow this index. Note that the Vanguard Total International Stock Index also includes a small (approximately 10 percent) exposure to the emerging markets, a useful diversifier. Putting a quarter of your money in one of these funds lessens your bet on a single country and currency—the U.S. dollar.

Table 5.3 International Index Funds		
Fund	**Ticker**	**Expense**
Fidelity Spartan International Index	FSIIX	0.10%
Vanguard Tax-Managed International Index	VTMGX	0.35%
iShares EAFE	EFA	0.35%
Vanguard Developed Markets Index	VDMIX	0.35%
Vanguard Total International Stock Index	VGTSX	0.36%
TIAA-CREF International Equity	TIINX	0.49%

We would have loved to include the investments discussed in these two points in our analysis, but unfortunately, there isn't enough data on U.S. inflation-protected bonds as an asset class to make long-term inferences from them. The foreign stocks underperformed the American ones during the '90s, but that was during the rise of the NASDAQ bubble and the collapse of Japan's economy, so it isn't a rock-solid baseline from which to extrapolate, either.

While modifying your portfolio in these ways will undoubtedly throw off our calculations somewhat, we think that they'll still be in the same ballpark. If it does throw them off, we believe it's likely to do so in the right direction.

As before, we think that you might be better off avoiding the closed-end funds (EFA and TIP) on these lists for now, so you won't have to pay commissions to reinvest your dividends.

The thinking man's couch potato portfolio looks like Figure 5.2.

Figure 5.2: The Thinking Man's Couch Potato Portfolio

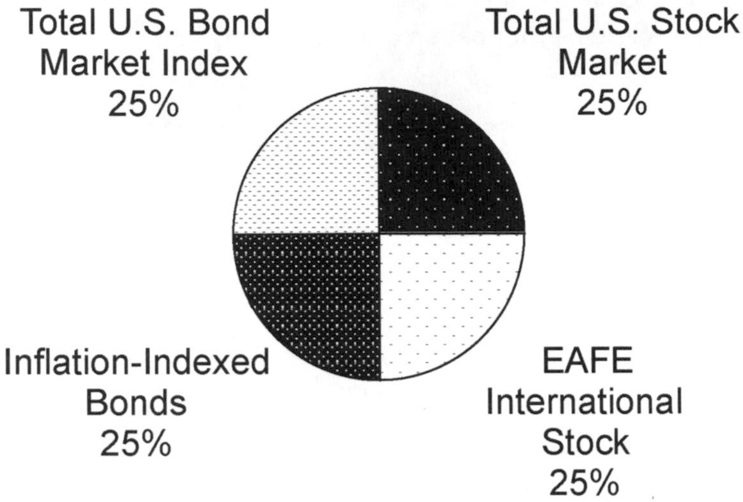

Total U.S. Bond
Market Index
25%

Total U.S. Stock
Market
25%

Inflation-Indexed
Bonds
25%

EAFE
International
Stock
25%

Asset Allocation

We like the 50–50 stock/bond allocation, and we think it's good for everyone. Unless you know that you have a better idea, we recommend that you stick to it.

The old saying about asset allocation is that your portfolio should grow more conservative as you grow older. One way that you may be advised to do this is by having a percentage of stocks in your portfolio equal to your age subtracted from 100. In other words, a 20-year-old should have 80 percent stocks, a 60-year-old should have 40 percent stocks, and an 80-year-old should have 20 percent stocks. It sounds catchy, but this is wrong for two reasons.

First, as you've seen, a 65-year-old must plan for a 30- or 40-year retirement. *The new retirees are still long-term investors.* If you invest only 35 percent in equities at this age, your portfolio is unlikely to grow enough to support a lifestyle-sustaining rate of withdrawal. Only the very rich can afford this degree of caution (for that matter, they can also afford to invest extremely aggressively). The rich are different from the rest of us—they have more money, as Hemingway said.

Second, the investment risk you can afford to take doesn't slope evenly downward throughout your lifetime, as the "subtract from 100" recipe implies. *Early retirement is by far the most dangerous time for retirees.* Steep losses here can doom your plans, forcing you to sell deeply depreciated assets in order to survive. This means that these investments will never have a chance to compound and grow later, so they'll never climb out of their slump. When you're 90 years old, you can invest more aggressively and still weather a downturn, since the same portfolio only has to carry you over for a shorter period of time.

Despite all this, we have no quarrel with the standard 60/40 stock/bond allocation routinely recommended by investment managers. We'd only point out that it's based on the analysis of the U.S. market in the 20th century, when stocks were for the most part quite cheap and bonds weren't. And in fact, Elroy Dimson, Paul Marsh, and Mike Staunton, writing in *Triumph of the Optimists: 101 Years of Global Investment Returns,* conclude that stocks have performed better than bonds in the past by a narrower margin than previously believed: "Taking the evidence of other countries and of a lower prospective equity premium, the apparent superiority of equities will in future years be attenuated" (p. 209). For this reason, we think that parking half your money in stocks and half in bonds is a perfectly sensible approach. If you want to tilt the allocation to overweight stocks up to 60 percent of your total portfolio, we'll look the other way.

Another factor influencing allocation is that financial planners are legally required to inquire about your investment "risk tolerance." Unfortunately, this concept is irrelevant to proper portfolio management. Imagine that you describe yourself as extremely low in risk tolerance and your adviser dutifully invests your portfolio 100 percent in T-bills. You may be at low risk of losing money month to month, but you are at a drastically *high* risk of running out of money during retirement. Or imagine that you describe yourself as a "devil-may-care adventurer who laughs in the face of danger." Does this mean that your adviser should put 100 percent of your money in tech stocks?

Asking an investor about risk tolerance is like a doctor asking a patient with a broken leg about "cast tolerance"—a stupid question with an irrelevant answer. You need to do the *correct* thing, not the feel-good thing.

With the couch potato portfolio, however, you never have to worry about your investment decisions again. You will own a little bit of everything, and will do as well as the markets allow. You won't have to follow the financial press and its passing parade of hucksters, so you can tune it all out and spend your time with your family or reading good books.

Portfolio Rebalancing

Experts are forever telling you to rebalance your portfolio every year, but your authors don't share the general enthusiasm for this ritual. We think it's better to do this only when your investment proportions get significantly out of alignment. Our projections here all assume that the 50 percent stock and 50 percent bond portfolio is rebalanced when it's off by 10 percent—for example, when it gets to be 60/40 or 40/60. If you're adding to your savings every year, you can always use the new money to shore up whichever side is lagging. We suspect that it wouldn't matter that much even if you didn't rebalance until it got to 70/30 or 30/70. The one exception is when you get close to retirement, and we'll tell you more about that later on in this chapter.

Market Timing

In *Yes, You Can Time the Market!,* we argued that it made more sense for investors to buy stocks when they were cheaply valued than to shovel their money into the market's open maw year after year. Our Website even tracks the various fundamentals so that you can see whether right now seems to be an advantageous time to buy.

However, the need for savings is so dramatic that virtually any program is better than none. Dollar-cost averaging into the market is a brilliant, five-star strategy compared to sidetracking your disposable income into current consumption. It's vastly more important that you save regularly than that you hit on the perfect investment plan.

The prudent couch potatoes will put half of their money into the stock and bond markets each year, rebalancing in the process.

However, we're going to mention an alternative strategy that has higher risks but possibly higher rewards: Buying more of what's cheap by historical standards is one way to squeeze as much return from your investment dollar as you can.

Imagine that two investors climbed into a time machine and went back to January 1, 1976, which by coincidence happens to be the date that Lehman Brothers first began compiling their Aggregate Bond Index (your authors are indebted to Lehman Brothers Global Family of Indices for providing us with data on its returns). One of these investors is a strict believer in dollar-cost averaging, so he immediately puts $50 into the total stock market index fund and $50 in the total bond market index fund. (Okay, so they didn't exist back then. Neither does the time machine! We're just supposing here. . . .)

Anyway, every month thereafter for the next 29 years, the dollar-cost averager repeats this ritual, adjusting his contribution for inflation, but otherwise splitting it evenly between stocks and bonds. He also rebalances his holdings between the two funds at the end of each year. By a stroke of good fortune, he pays no commissions, taxes, or fees of any kind along the way, and by August 2004 his account has grown to $360,809.

The other investor grabbed a copy of *Yes, You Can Time the Market!* before climbing into the time machine. Struck by its good sense, he realized that he was sitting on a potential gold mine. Instead of dollar-cost averaging like his time-traveling pal, at the beginning of each month he checked the market indicators (the kind that you can view on **www.stein-demuth.com**). If the market looked undervalued by any of these metrics, he put the entirety of his $100 into the total stock market fund. If the stock market looked overvalued at the start of the month, he put all his money instead into the total bond market fund. Like his colleague, he also adjusted his $100 contribution for inflation every month and dodged all taxes, fees, and commissions; but unlike his pal, he never rebalanced. By August 2004, he'd amassed $417,413.

Figure 5.3 shows the course of these two fortunes.

Figure 5.3: Market Timing vs. Dollar Cost Averaging into the Couch Potato Portfolio

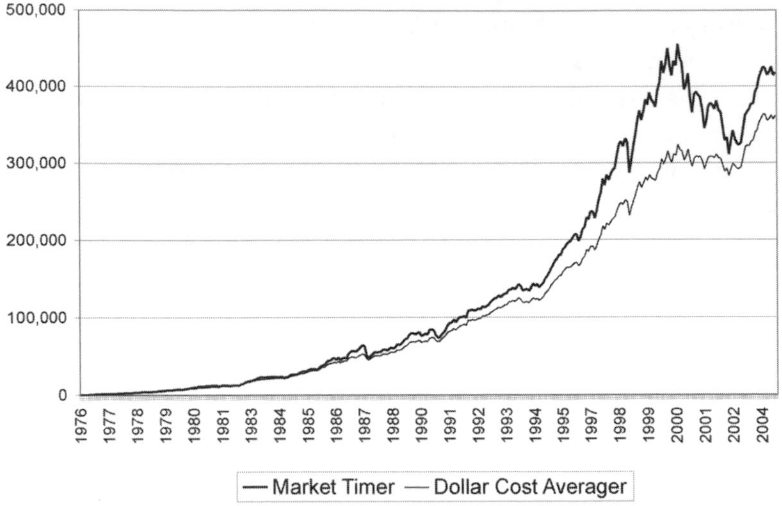

— Market Timer — Dollar Cost Averager

Before you become a born-again market timer, pay special attention to the years 2000 to 2003. Notice how the market timer watched the floor fall out from under him during this time, while the dollar-cost averager (cushioned by his heftier bond position) had a smoother ride. If you'd retired as the market timer in 2000, you would have had plenty of sleepless nights. Even so, note that at no time did the market timer actually have less money than his friend. He had to drink more Pepto-Bismol to get it, though.

An Intermediate Position

What if you like this market-timing idea but aren't sure that you want to bet the farm on it? In that case, consider the "lite" version. Consult the metrics on our Website before you make your periodic investment (monthly, quarterly, annually, or whenever). If stocks are undervalued by any of our indicators, put 75 percent of the money you were going to invest into stocks, and 25 percent into bonds. If stocks appear overvalued, put 25 percent into stocks anyway (just to be safe) and place the remaining 75 percent in the bond market.

An investor who followed this strategy since 1976 with an inflation-adjusted $100 each month would have made $387,010—a tad better than the dollar-cost averager above.

Later, you'll see that this market timing seems to add value on the withdrawal side as well.

Where to Hold Your Accounts

To get ahead of ourselves for a moment, the general thinking is that after you retire, you should tap your taxable accounts first so that your tax-deferred holdings will have that much longer to compound, untouched by the IRS. Following this line of thinking, you may be told that you should clone your overall portfolio in both the taxable and tax-deferred editions, but this is wrong.

The advantage of letting your tax-deferred accounts compound for a few extra years until you're forced to start making withdrawals at age 70½ is overridden by the disadvantage of having to hold bonds in your taxable account over the entire life of the portfolio, where their coupons are taxed at your standard marginal rate year after year.

The smart move is to *hold all your bonds in tax-deferred accounts—* that is, IRAs, 401(k)s, 457 plans, and the like. Hold your stock funds in taxable accounts, where their dividends and long-term capital gains will be taxed at a lower rate. It should go without saying that you'll always want to max out your employee accounts to take advantage of any matching contributions from your employer. This is found money, so don't leave it on the table.

Here's another piece of advice that goes against the grain of popular wisdom: *Don't put all your savings into tax-deferred accounts.* These monies are going to be taxed at marginal rates upon withdrawal, and who knows how those rates will change? Recall that they've been more than 90 percent during the past century. When you keep your money in taxable accounts, however, it's pay-as-you-go. Sure, your dividends, coupons, and capital gains are taxed along the way (at lower rates, we hope), but after that, the money is yours (at least, after you pay the taxes on any long-term realized gains).

Some pundits think that you should load up on real estate (such as your house), since there's a substantial one-time capital gains exclusion when it's sold. The problem is that all of this can change with the stroke of a congressional pen, so don't place all your bets on any one option, such as taxable accounts, tax-deferred accounts, or even real estate. Who knows where the tax man's heaviest hand will land? Even Roth IRAs could end up being taxed. Spread your assets around. Diversify the types of accounts, as well as the assets themselves.

For accounts that you manage yourself, a discount brokerage is a cheap way to purchase closed-end mutual funds, while open-end choices can be had directly from the sponsoring investment company for free. Vanguard is the historical cost king, but in a blatant grab for market share, Fidelity has recently pared expenses on some of their index funds (such as their total stock market fund and EAFE stock fund) to a scant 0.10 percent. But Vanguard is so good at the index game that it has better total returns, even after its slightly higher expenses.

Fidelity also has excellent online discount-brokerage services for picking the other stocks or funds that you might need. Getting everything on one statement makes it easier to keep track of your finances, especially for people who aren't devotees of Microsoft's Money or Intuit's Quicken.

For your tax-deferred accounts at work, you're stuck with whatever plan your employer's chosen. More and more often, large companies are being sensible enough to use Vanguard, Fidelity, T. Rowe Price, or Dimensional Fund Advisors. If this is the case where you work, you're in clover. But small employers often have to scrounge to cobble a plan together, taking whatever they can get. In this scenario, you'll probably be saddled with funds that have high expenses. Tragic, but true.

In implementing the couch potato portfolio (or its cousin, the "thinking man's" version), you'll want to stuff your 401(k) with bonds. Look hard for any fund that tracks the total bond market or, God willing, inflation-indexed bonds. Absent that, pick whatever fund holds intermediate-term bonds. Don't hold long bonds and don't hold cash or "stable value" funds. If there's nothing in this ballpark, then punt and pick whatever S&P 500 index fund (or better, total stock market index fund) they offer. You'll just have to make the best of it.

On the Cusp of Retirement

When you get within five years of retirement, it's time to take a careful look at where you stand and where you're headed.

Minimizing potential losses to your portfolio becomes all-important at this point. For that reason, even if you've been an indifferent rebalancer in the past, we suggest that you start to rebalance your portfolio annually. The idea isn't to boost your returns but to decrease risk. If your account is 80 percent stocks and 20 percent bonds, it will be less likely to take a big dive if you reposition it to 50 percent stocks and 50 percent bonds. Remember the free fall that our market timer experienced from 2000 to 2003? He could have avoided some of this turbulence if he'd rebalanced before 2000 hit.

Advisors sometimes recommend putting your money into some extremely conservative investment once your retirement nest egg is topped off. Our problem with this is that for your nest egg to really be topped off, you need about 35 times your annual expenditures in savings. So unless you've amassed a personal fortune of this magnitude, you're going to have to ride with the markets.

107

A 70-year-old retiree is still a long-term investor, and needs to get a market rate of return from his nest egg to fund his retirement. If you decide to play it safe and go to T-bills with less than 35 times your needed self-generated income in savings, you may be setting yourself up to run out of money later. However, it remains true that the more savings you have, the less risk you have to take.

If you've been purchasing stocks within a taxable account, we recommend that you read the chapter on income investing. When you get within a few years of your retirement date, start diverting some of your new savings away from the U.S. total stock market and Europe, Australia, and Far East indexes, and toward two types of equities that we haven't discussed yet: high-dividend stocks and real estate investment trusts. If you are buying your stocks within a tax-deferred account, you can skip this step for now, because you can always buy and sell within the account later without triggering any tax consequences.

This brings us to the threshold of retirement itself, the subject of the next chapter.

■ ■ ■

CHAPTER 6

The Retiree's Paradox

s a new retiree, you'll face a paradox: On the one hand, you'll be ready to party. Starting from day one, you'll want to do many things that cost a lot of money, such as play golf and travel, for starters. What's more, you'll be itching to do these things right away, because you might not be up to it later. When you're 90, you may not feel like scaling Kilimanjaro—a few premium cable channels and a bag of Cheetos ought to take care of it. At the beginning, though, you'll wanna dance.

Unfortunately, there's a hitch: For the portfolios we've described in the previous chapters, it's just the reverse of a new retiree's instincts. Take a look at Figure 6.1. It plots the course of 10,000 sample nest eggs of $1 million each, invested in the couch potato portfolio, through 25 years of retirement. We've withdrawn $50,000 the first year (5 percent) and every year thereafter, adjusting this amount for inflation. Note that for the purposes of this experiment, it wouldn't matter if we started with $100,000 and withdrew an inflation-adjusted $5,000 (also 5 percent) each year.

Figure 6.1: Monte Carlo Portfolio Withdrawal Simulations

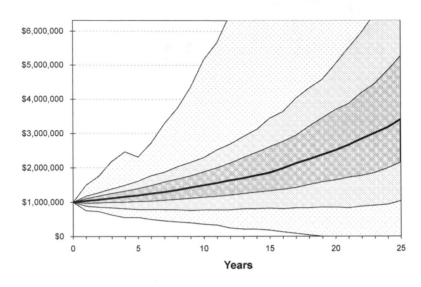

The graph shows that you're likely to end up with a pile of money—more than you could dream of spending on the Home Shopping Network as a remote-wielding nonagenarian (although you might end up spending a good chunk of it if you are channel surfing in a nursing home). This likely accumulation of capital shows the power of the markets at work.

But not everyone is so fortunate. You cannot assume that you're going to get a straight line amortization from your investment accounts, as if the stock market is paying down a mortgage every year. In reality, the markets are up some years and down others. *As sellers of securities, the particular sequence of returns that you get will have an enormous impact on your outcome.*

Let's look at three cases. These all represent possible scenarios having the same average variation of returns that the U.S. stock and bond markets display. Our retiree starts with $1 million, taking out an inflation-adjusted $50,000 at the start of each year. Here's how the best case out of 10,000 ran:

Table 6.1: Best Case out of 10,000		
Year	Portfolio Returns	End-of-Year Balance
1	94%	$1,844,111
2	21%	$2,168,454
3	44%	$3,043,881
4	5%	$3,156,496
5	38%	$4,287,345

In year one, this guy's up 94 percent! The next, he gains another 21 percent, and 44 percent the year after that. Talk about a hot hand: After 25 years, this Gladstone Gander has $70,225,296 in the bank.

How did he get so rich? The secret is scoring big early on. After just a few years, he doubled his initial stake, which gave him the entire rest of the time to expose this increased kitty to market forces. He won the race because he had such a huge head start.

The median case isn't quite so impressive, as you can see in Table 6.2.

111

Table 6.2: Median Case out of 10,000		
Year	Portfolio Returns	End-of-Year Balance
1	7%	$1,018,534
2	8%	$1,047,948
3	7%	$1,071,872
4	8%	$1,104,270
5	8%	$1,136,694

This person gets inflation-adjusted returns from his combined stock and bond portfolio in the range of 7 to 8 percent, allowing it to grow nicely even after he pulls out his $50,000 every 12 months. At the end of 25 years, his estate is worth a handsome $2,441,162.

Which brings us to the worst case out of 10,000, shown in Table 6.3. Read it and weep.

Table 6.3: Worst Case out of 10,000		
Year	Portfolio Returns	End-of-Year Balance
1	-35%	$613,957
2	-8%	$517,244
3	-17%	$388,414
4	-12%	$296,828
5	-21%	$194,093

This poor schnook is down 35 percent in year one; and as if that weren't awful enough, he gets clobbered with an 8 percent loss in year two, a 17 percent loss in year three, and minus 12 percent in year four. With luck like this, he never makes it to the finish line, but instead runs out of money at the end of the first quarter in year 11.

Looking back at all 10,000 simulations, 21 percent of these retirees had to dip into principal to survive, and more than 7 percent had the horrible experience of "negative mortality," or running out of money before they ran out of life. The possibility of dipping into principal is a foregone conclusion for all but the richest of the boomer generation. It's the prospect of running out of money that should get your attention.

Here's nature's cruel joke on retirees: *You'll probably have all the money in the world later, when you can't spend it, but you only get a pittance at the beginning, when you really want it.*

Which means the $64 question is: *How can you channel the money from the pot of gold that likely awaits you at the end of retirement into your lifestyle today?* That is, how do you siphon the money from the bank in Tomorrowland to your bank on Main Street? How can you bring Oz back to Kansas?

You have to proceed carefully, because if you spend even a little bit too much money today, the fortune waiting for you can disappear into the phantom zone, and you'll run out of money.

From Nest Egg to Goose Egg

Something about the example we just posed may have bothered you. It was the assumption that you could live off 5 percent of your nest egg. Does this mean that if you're a millionaire, you can only draw $50,000 per year, and then you have to pay taxes on top of that? This is hardly the stuff of champagne wishes and caviar dreams.

The answer is that you'll get 5 percent—if you're lucky. According to historical studies, the most that you can withdraw from your nest egg is actually closer to 4 percent, and even this rate may be too ambitious.

These studies all look at one set of investment runs: those that actually occurred from 1926 to 1995. The 20th century was a stupendous bull market, but just because that's the way things went in the past doesn't mean that's what's going to happen from 2005 to 2099.

Figure 6.2 shows the results of 1,000 reasonably diversified retirement portfolios withdrawing 5 percent each year. Of those that ended up going broke within 25 years, in nearly all cases there were sirens sounding long before the end: More than half the portfolios that were down 10 percent from their initial levels after two years went bust, and more than 60 percent of the portfolios that slid 10 percent after three years went south. For those that decreased this much after four years, the failure rate climbed to over 80 percent.

If your nest egg drops a total of 10 percent from where you started within the first five years of your retirement, wake up and smell the Geritol. Take whatever steps are necessary to reduce your expenditures. A 4 percent withdrawal of your initial nest egg level, adjusted for inflation in following years, would seem a prudent upper limit until your portfolio recovers.

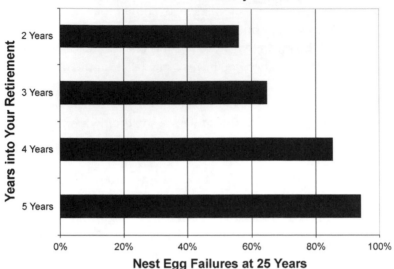

Figure 6.2: Nest Egg Failure Rate for
Portfolios Down 10% in Early Retirement

Note that these problem scenarios are singing the same sad song as our guy with the worst-case returns shown in Table 6.3. His huge initial losses coupled with his ongoing need for cash—forcing him to sell low—meant that there was no hope for him to get out of the hole. With only a few more bad years, he was completely wiped out. However, his situation was preventable: He should have rebalanced, and he should have pared back his withdrawals after his catastrophic start.

If you don't have sufficient savings to begin with (as is often the case), how can you maximize your income in early retirement, when you want it the most, without jeopardizing your final years? How can you siphon surplus capital from tomorrow and convert it into spending money today? This is the central financial issue faced by the baby-boom generation.

Investing for Growth in Retirement

Investing for growth has a soft underbelly: It's highly vulnerable to a bear market arriving shortly after you retire. This puts your portfolio into a hole that it can never crawl out of, since then you must sell your assets in order to make ends meet, rather than letting the power of compound interest save you over the long run. Early retirement is the diciest time because of this sensitive dependence on initial conditions.

Think of it this way: If you're driving from Los Angeles for an appointment in San Francisco and get caught in a two-hour traffic jam on Highway 101 just as you leave town, it really doesn't matter how fast you drive later on, because you're not going to make it. This is why the worst-case scenarios have the unfortunate investor retiring the day before the stock-market crash on October 29, 1929; retiring in 1966 or 2000 would have produced a similar knuckle-biting experience. New retirees have an exquisite vulnerability to loss, precisely at the moment when they'd most like to forget their cares and cruise around the world.

Former Fidelity Magellan Fund guru Peter Lynch gave some famously bad advice in *Beating the Street,* and then repeated it in *Worth* magazine. He suggested that an insouciant retiree could invest 100 percent in stocks, pocket a tidy 7 percent every year, and still end up with a pile of money after two decades.

The problem was (and is) that even though this outcome is possible—even likely—it is by no means inevitable. Even when average stock market returns are high, their variability can be punishing. A number of scenarios betting on the Lynch strategy have the hapless retiree going bankrupt.

Of course, you could sidestep this problem by avoiding risky assets like stocks that can crater in value. But doing this diminishes your upside potential, and the pot of gold at the end of retirement sprouts wings and flies away.

On the other hand, if you hold too many equities at the beginning, the pot of gold disappears if a bear market hits. You've already seen how retirees must plan for maximum—not average—life expectancies, which are far longer today than at any point in history. The longer the tour of duty your growth-oriented portfolio must give service, the bigger it's likely to be in the end, but the less you can withdraw early on lest the whole edifice collapse. This calls for sensitive management.

We set up our projections about how much you should be saving based on the historical performance of the couch potato portfolio (1979–2004) and the withdrawal rates it should sustain. You should be able to manage all of your retirement savings and withdrawals from the couch potato portfolio alone. But that said, growth investing does not have to be the whole show. You can also invest directly for income, as we discuss next.

■ ■ ■

CHAPTER 7

Investing for Income

The alternative to investing for growth is investing for income. Conveniently, your authors have written a book on this very subject: *Yes, You Can Be a Successful Income Investor!* In some ways, it could be considered a companion piece to this opus.

Investing for income is one way of trading future growth for current cash. It means that you'll likely have a smaller pot of gold at the end of the rainbow in exchange for higher income today—a trade-off many retirees will gladly make. This strategy involves buying income-paying securities that have limited growth prospects but pay a high coupon or dividend in compensation. These can include bonds like those in the Lehman Brothers Aggregate and the inflation-protected securities that you already own (if you've followed our advice from earlier chapters). You can also look to certain segments of the stock market that your total stock market index contains in small measure, but here you would emphasize: high-dividend stocks and real estate investment trusts.

Figure 7.1 shows how the recommended income portfolio is allocated, with the proportions tilted 60/40 in favor of bonds.

Figure 7.1: A Diversified Income Portfolio

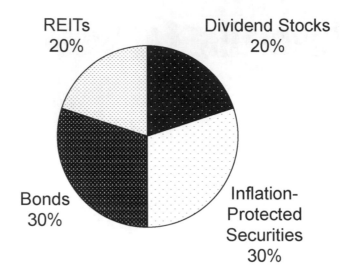

REITs
20%

Dividend Stocks
20%

Bonds
30%

Inflation-
Protected
Securities
30%

118

This heavier bond allocation makes the portfolio more conserva-tive, as does the presence of stodgy dividend stocks such as banks and utilities. These are more stable than most growth stocks and make for a portfolio that fluctuates less month to month than the couch potato portfolio does. This makes retirees (who tend to be a conservative lot) happy.

The ingredients for a vanilla income portfolio are profiled in Table 7.1.

Table 7.1: A Conservative Income Portfolio

Percent	Asset	Ticker	Yield	Expense
REITs				
20%	Vanguard REIT Index VIPERS	VNQ	4.90%	0.18%
STOCKS				
20%	iShares Dow Jones Select Dividend Fund	DVY	3.26%	0.40%
TIPS				
30%	iShares Lehman TIPS	TIP	4.84%	0.20%
BONDS				
30%	iShares Lehman Aggregate	AGG	3.69%	0.20%

The portfolio is reasonably diversified, is somewhat protected from inflation, and allows for the prospect of capital appreciation (and hence a growth in yield that should keep pace with your living expenses). If future performance is at all like recent history, this is a very conservative choice, with the prospect of losing money in any given year being about 1 in 20. Four mutual funds comprise it, and you should already own two of them: the Lehman Brothers Aggregate Bond Index and the TIPS. The others are the iShares Dow Jones Select Dividend Index (ticker DVY), which holds a pool of the highest consistent dividend-paying stocks in the Wilshire 5000, and an index fund of real estate investment trusts (REITs) from Vanguard (ticker VNQ). These trusts own commercial real estate from various sectors of the economy and pass nearly all of the rents along to shareholders, as demanded by the REIT operating structure. The dividends are high because they're leveraged investments (just as your investment in your house is leveraged when you have a mortgage).

Considering all of this, should you put a portion of your portfolio into an income account once you retire? Very possibly you should. Let's explore the issues.

Possibilities for Increased Yield

The yield will no doubt be different by the time you read this, but as of this writing these funds give you a 4.2 percent current yield. This is already a bit better than the minimum allowance suggested by academics (4 percent) for drawing down your retirement portfolio, and it involves less risk.

If interest rates have gone up by the time you read this, however, these rates will have changed as well. If you can get a 6 percent yield from your money-market fund today, don't assume that this portfolio is obsolete, since it should be yielding more as well. Its net asset value will fluctuate, and it probably won't grow as much as the couch potato portfolio, but the idea is to ignore the price variations and spend the dividend checks.

For example, REITs have been on a tear for several years and may be destined to fall in value. However, we still expect that tenants will continue paying their rents and the trusts will keep passing them along. Ignore the month-to-month vicissitudes and focus on the rising, inflation-beating stream of payments they can direct your way.

A retiree might very well elect to put half of his assets into an income approach. This would diversify his approach across two strategies (growth and income). If one didn't work as expected, the other would be a backup system for at least half of his income stream. While these strategies have a short history, the correlation between them is quite low.

Readers of *Yes, You Can Be a Successful Income Investor!* will be aware that more aggressive income approaches are also possible. For example, by taking the trouble to select individual income stocks and REITs, you might add another percentage point to the yield of the conservative portfolio shown here, and by using leveraged bond or dividend funds, you might add yet another percentage point or more on top of that (with added risks, naturally).

If you used our back-of-the-envelope method, up until this point we've either had you save with the expectation that eventually you'll be drawing down your nest egg at a rate of 5 percent (using conservative assumptions) or 6.2 percent (using moderate assumptions), as embedded in Tables 3.3 and 3.4 (pages 66 and 68). These rates of withdrawal are the focus of our next chapter, but for now we'll point out that they're more than the 4.2 percent this conservative income portfolio presently pays.

To move the income portfolio out to a 5 percent yield today, you'll need to dial in a set of holdings with a higher return (there are plenty of ideas about how to do this in our other book, such as buying some individual high-dividend stocks and real estate investment trusts). That way you'll maintain your targeted income level during your initial phase of retirement. To get a 6.2 percent yield today, you'll have to add some leveraged funds.

Whatever the withdrawal rate you decide upon from your couch potato portfolio, you'll have to tinker with your income portfolio to match it. Otherwise, you won't get the full amount from your nest egg that you're expecting.

We can't tell you in advance what the basic income portfolio will yield on the day that you retire. You'll just have to see what the funds that compose it are yielding at that point, and then take the necessary steps to adjust it until it approximately matches your selected withdrawal rate from your couch potato portfolio. This will be a little more work, but the diversification benefit should be worth it. After all, you're retired, so you should have time to pay more attention to your money. As surprising as it may seem right now, it could well be that the income portfolio will have a *higher* annual yield than your target initial withdrawal rate from the couch potato portfolio.

Let's turn back the clock to see how this generic income portfolio might have looked over the past 20 years. Table 7.2 (page 122) shows a portfolio constructed along the same lines that we've already discussed, with 20 percent invested a REIT index fund, 20 percent in the stock of an electrical utility (Consolidated Edison is used here as a proxy for high-dividend stocks in general), and 60 percent in a ten-year Treasury bond. This is *not* a diversified portfolio, we're just using it as an illustration.

Table 7.2: Historical Yield of Income Instruments				
	REITs	**CON ED**	**10-Year Bond**	**Portfolio**
1985	7.1%	13.8%	11.6%	11.1%
1990	8.4%	5.9%	7.9%	7.6%
1995	7.7%	7.8%	7.8%	7.8%
2000	8.7%	6.1%	6.5%	6.9%
2005	4.7%	5.3%	4.2%	4.5%

This very simple portfolio has yielded 7.6 percent on average over the past 20 years—far more than you could have safely withdrawn from your couch potato growth portfolio at the start of your retirement. This is almost exactly what you could get from an aggressive income portfolio today—albeit at greater risk.

As interest rates go up, so should the yields on income-producing securities, making the income portfolio more attractive. Unfortunately, the process of getting from here to there won't be painless, because a rising interest rate environment is no friend to either stocks or bonds.

How to Set Up Your Accounts

It's most convenient to keep your income account separate from your couch potato one, because you're going to be using them differently. With the couch potato account, you're going to be breaking off a little piece every year and selling it to get cash for living expenses. Your income account is much simpler: All you do is cash the coupon and dividend checks and spend the money.

If you've kept your savings in tax-free accounts prior to retirement, you can buy and sell securities with impunity, so detouring your portfolio into these income funds is simplicity itself, with no tax consequences and minimal transaction costs.

Given the alternatives, it's generally best to keep your dividend stocks in a taxable account, where the dividends will be taxed at the top 15 percent rate upon withdrawal. Inflation-protected Treasuries, on the other hand, need to be in tax-deferred accounts to guard against the possibility of having to pay the IRS taxes on any phantom income. REITs are also tax-intensive since their dividends (except for the portion that represents depreciation) are mostly taxed at your marginal rates. These trusts are better off in tax-deferred accounts, because you always have the option of purchasing municipal bonds for your taxable accounts.

If all of your money that can be taxed consists of assets that have greatly appreciated over the years, you'll have to weigh the benefits of moving a portion of them over to the income approach against the tax costs of realizing these gains on the first day of your retirement. There is a lot to be said for postponing paying taxes as long as possible. As we suggested earlier, a better strategy in the few years just before retirement might be to shuttle your stock purchases to buying REITs and high-dividend stocks instead of the total U.S. stock market and EAFE index funds.

Up to this point in your investing career, you've had everything set up to reinvest all dividends and capital gains, but you now need to contact the mutual-fund companies and arrange to have these distributed to your account instead. This happens automatically when you own exchange-traded funds, such as the dividend fund (DVY) or the REIT fund (VNQ); and if you have your bonds in an exchange-traded fund (TIP or AGG, for example) these are also distributed.

Next, arrange to have the cash balance in these accounts (taxable or tax-deferred) electronically transferred into your checking account every quarter. Don't use a wire transfer (which might cost $15 a pop), but an ACH electronic transfer (which is free). If you can make this happen automatically, so much the better.

Final step: Spend the money.

That's all there is to the income account. With the generic portfolio above, you can "set it and forget it." If you've bought one of the more advanced portfolios that rely on specific stocks or REITs, you'll have to pay some ongoing attention to it in order to make sure that they remain appropriate investments—not a bad hobby for a new retiree. And by all means rebalance within the account if the allocation gets significantly out of alignment from where you started, especially if you can do so without undue tax consequences.

You can also rebalance between the income and couch potato accounts—but maybe don't bother if this means you have to forklift over a bale of money to Uncle Sam in the process. Also remember that if your income account is held within an IRA, you'll have to begin taking substantially equal payments from it as of age 70½. Check IRS Publication 590 for details. You may have to sell off some of your assets each year in order to reach this minimum distribution amount if the dividends and coupons alone don't get you up to the minimum distribution levels.

With the income account, you just set it up, monitor it, and cash the checks. This is an optional approach to retirement income—not required—but if you can set it up it efficiently, this can really diversify your income stream. Using your couch potato account in retirement is another story . . . the subject of our next chapter, in fact.

■ ■ ■

CHAPTER 8

Drawing Down Your Couch Potato Portfolio

B efore we get to the question of how much you can withdraw from these accounts, there's something you need to do immediately . . . .

Move Your Accounts!

While you were growing your nest egg, we assumed that most of your personal savings were captive in your 401(k) account. These have notoriously poor choices and high expenses. We also assumed that you'd be shelling out one percent of your assets every year in management fees for even the least costly options. That's way too much, but there was really nothing you could do about it.

Once you've retired, however, it's a new ball game. You can roll over your 401(k) to an investment account at Vanguard, Fidelity, T. Rowe Price, or some other low-cost provider. Just be sure that you don't touch the money yourself, or the IRS will come after you. Have the check from your plan sponsor made out directly to the low-fee mutual fund company you choose.

If you make this switch, your fund fees going forward can drop to 0.20 percent annually. Of course, you can choose not to take action, leaving the money in your high-expense plan and paying your cash to the sponsor in the form of high fees—or you can move your assets to a low-fee sponsor and pay yourself instead. We're going to assume that you'll take the latter course. If you elect *not* to do this, you'll have to trim your withdrawals every year by the difference between whatever you're paying in management fees at present and the 0.20 percent we're assuming you will be charged going forward.

You'll find that moving your accounts is a breeze: One simple form will do it. These mutual-fund companies are eager for your business, and they make the transfer as easy as pie.

The other thing to consider now is your pension plan. If you work for the government and your plan is rock solid, then stand pat. If you have a built-in cost-of-living allowance and your plan otherwise appears to be in good shape, we might advise you to keep that one where it is, too. But in other cases, instead of trusting your benefit plan to keep paying you for the rest of your life, you might want to add the lump sum they're offering to your other assets and manage them yourself. Absent an inflation adjustment, keep in mind that the purchasing power of your initial payout will probably be cut in half over the course of your retirement. Calculate your income stream both ways, and see which one works better for you (*if* they give you this payout option, which they probably won't).

Remember, however, that if you decide to roll over a lump sum to an IRA, you must indeed *roll over* the money, not *withdraw* it and then deposit it in an IRA yourself. It you touch it, you'll have the IRS knocking at your door.

Got the accounts transferred? Good. Let's move on.

How Much Can You Withdraw from Your Growth Portfolio Each Year?

The quick answer to this question is: It depends.

Before you start throwing rotten tomatoes at us, we need to explain how we arrived at our conclusions. It all depends on how much income you want early on in retirement, and how comfortable you are taking the risks involved to get it. We want to quantify the trade-offs for you so that you can make an informed decision.

Our numbers are not rocket science, but they are an offshoot of the Manhattan Project of World War II, when the United States was on a quest to develop the atom bomb. Physicists at Los Alamos needed to calculate neutron transport probabilities within the nuclear-reactor core by following one neutron at a time to determine when it might collide, scatter, or become absorbed, and so they came up with random simulation models to solve the problem. The code name for their solution was "Monte Carlo," after the elegant quarter in Monaco where the fancy casinos are located. Today, financial planners use Monte Carlo simulations to "stress test" portfolios.

While the historical record provides one way to back test a portfolio, such as was done in the famous Trinity Study (named after Trinity University in San Antonio, not the atom-bomb test site) that examined the years 1926 to 1995, the past only provides one scenario. Monte Carlo methodology allows us to examine thousands of possible scenarios. Here your authors are indebted to the brilliant chartered financial analyst Bill Swerbenski, developer of the Portfolio Survival Simulator software on which we ran our calculations.

Since we have nearly 30 years of historical data on the performance of the couch potato portfolio, we plugged these returns (along with their variability and correlations) into our Monte Carlo simulator, spun the wheel, and saw how many of them were still standing years later at the end of retirement.

Figure 8.1 (page 128) displays the percentage of the couch potato growth portfolio that you can withdraw each year of retirement, at varying rates of risk. If you're reading this book in the library, this is the page you should take to the Xerox machine.

Most researchers who address this issue have searched for the initial withdrawal amount, adjusted by inflation thereafter, which will safely sustain your nest egg over your projected life span—a "one size fits all" approach. Using this method, the usual answer hovers around an initial 4 percent withdrawal from your diversified stock-and-bond portfolio.

The problem is that you don't know in advance which path your particular investment returns will take. If you get great returns, you could safely pull out substantially more. The trade-off we propose is this: Reset this withdrawal amount every five years. In most cases, this should allow you to take more, both initially and along the way—although at the expense of having a smaller estate to leave behind later.

Figure 8.1: Couch Potato Portfolio Withdrawal Rates

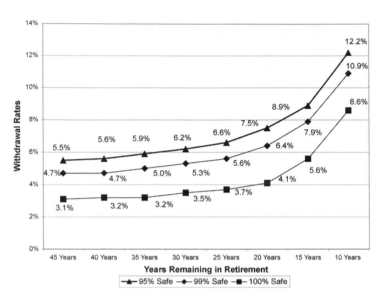

A glance at this graph makes two things clear: First, the longer that you postpone retirement, the more money you can safely withdraw. You can initially take out about 46 percent more from your growth portfolio if you're only planning to be retired for 25 years rather than 40.

Second, you pay a very high price for cleaving to 100 percent safety in early retirement. If you want to live in a world where no sequence out of 25,000 possibilities has you running out of money, you have to initially withdraw 43 percent less than you could if you were willing to accept a one percent chance of these portfolios going bust. And you have to make do with 55 percent less cash than if you were okay with a 5 percent chance of your nest egg prematurely disappearing.

While the very highest margin of safety is certainly desirable, you have to ask: Can I afford it? As an alternative, you might take on more risk, on the theory that if the markets turn against you and you're beset by losses early on, you'll take your lumps and retreat to a safer spending level.

However, one unavoidable effect of transporting more into present expenditure is that this reduces the value of your final estate, as shown in Figure 8.2.

Figure 8.2: Impact of Different Withdrawal Rates on Final Estate

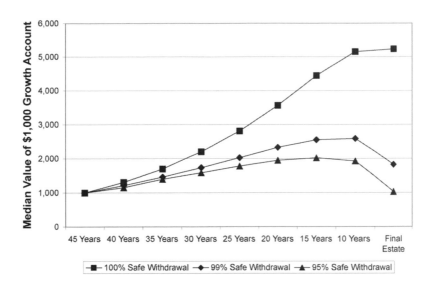

As you can see, taking an extra percentage point now has a big impact later. This isn't a problem (except possibly for your heirs); rather, it speaks to the success of the withdrawal program we've outlined. It's an efficient time machine for transferring funds from the hypothetical bank account of the future into purchasing power in the present . . . which is the whole point.

Be aware that these are median figures and intended for illustration only. Given the variability of investment returns, it's possible that your growth account and final estate will be considerably larger or smaller than those shown here. Nevertheless, if you adhere to the following steps, you're likely to do just fine.

How to Do It

Before we get into the nitty-gritty, we want you to keep this in mind: As you go along, you're going to be breaking your retirement into a succession of five-year periods, reevaluating and adjusting your withdrawal rate at the beginning of each new five-year plan. The changes to your withdrawal amount will be based on the remaining amount of time in your retirement, the performance of your underlying investment portfolio, and the rate of inflation. If you start to get bogged down in the details, just pause for a moment to refocus on those five-year periods, and you should be able to orient yourself.

And now, here are the mechanics of how to set up your withdrawal program:

1. Estimate the length of your retirement. Figure out where you're jumping in. If you want to assume a 99 percent degree of safety for longevity risk, assume that you'll live to age 105; while if you're comfortable with a 95 percent degree of longevity risk, drop that age to 100. If you're part of a couple, you can go to our Website for a link to a joint-longevity calculator (since two people live longer than one, on average). Subtract the age at which you retire from this maximum age to see how long your money will be supporting you. For purposes of this illustration, let's assume that you're planning a 35-year retirement.

2. Pick your initial withdrawal rate. Decide how much investment risk you're willing to take—that is, what percentage of portfolio withdrawal rates still have you financially solvent at the end. If you want a scenario in which 100 percent of portfolios are successful, you'll need to withdraw a fairly low percentage of your assets initially. But if you're willing to tolerate a one percent risk of running out of money before you run out of life (a 99 percent safety level), you'll be able to take out substantially more. *This has been the assumption behind the savings rates recommended in earlier chapters,* and we'll use it in this example as well.

However, if you're willing to accept a 5 percent risk (a 95 percent safety level), you can withdraw even more to start. Choosing the 95 percent safe-withdrawal level gives you more money initially, but probably less money later—even though the *percentage* withdrawals further out are still higher. Over the entire span of your retirement, you'll typically end up with more spending money overall by choosing the 99 percent safe original withdrawal rate. This is because more funds are left in the kitty early on to grow for later use.

3. Withdraw the money. Looking at Figure 8.1 (page 128), you'll see that a 35-year-retirement with a one percent chance of portfolio failure corresponds to an initial withdrawal rate of 5 percent. While this larger amount may not cause you to pop the champagne, it gets better over time, because with every year of retirement that passes, there's one fewer year that these accounts need to support you. But to begin, you'll withdraw 5 percent times the amount of money in your growth portfolio.

Even with something this simple, there's more than one way to do it. The method you choose can have a big impact on how your account grows. Here are a few options:

- You can sell half from your stock fund and half from your bond fund every year and have the proceeds transferred into your checking or money-market account.

- You can sell off proportionately from the stock and bond funds, with the aim of rebalancing the account back to 50-50 each year as you go. This is especially advisable in the first few years of your retirement.

- You can sell from the stock side in years when stocks are up and from the bond side when stocks are down (see "Retirement Withdrawal Strategies—Other Voices" in the Appendix).

- Best of all, in our opinion: You can try to add value by "timing the market"—a method we'll describe later in this chapter.

In any event, the sum that you withdraw by redeeming a portion of your various mutual funds (plus any dividends that you have coming in from your income account) is your "allowance" for the year. There's no harm in taking this money out on a quarterly basis, if you prefer. You may find it reassuring, however, to have all of the cash for the year in the bank—especially if you've budgeted your spending so that you won't blow through it too quickly.

4. Annual adjustments. The second year of your retirement, you'll withdraw the same dollar amount as the first year, but adjusted for the rate of inflation (which you can find at **www.stein-demuth.com**). For example, if you initially withdrew $30,000 and inflation was 3 percent during that year, you'd withdraw an extra $900 ($30,000 x 3 percent) at the start of the second year, or $30,900. This should keep your purchasing power even, but we do have two caveats:

1. *Do **not** add the inflation rate to the withdrawal rate to come up with some new figure. For example, you might think that a 5 percent withdrawal rate + 3 percent inflation = a new withdrawal rate of 8 percent—**not!***

2. *Do **not** multiply the initial withdrawal rate by the total value of your portfolio at the beginning of each of the next four years to determine how much cash to withdraw. Rather, pull out the same fixed dollar amount each year, adjusted for inflation in years two through four.*

132

For the next three years (retirement years three through five), do the same thing: Adjust your withdrawal amount by the rate of inflation as you go. If the rate of inflation averaged one percent during the second year, you'd withdraw an extra $309 ($30,900 x one percent) at the start of year three. Every 12 months for years two through five, you'll adjust your cumulative withdrawal by the rate of inflation.

If you get hit with a whammy of a loss in your portfolio during the first five years, cut back your withdrawal rate to what would have been an initial 4 percent safe level, adjusting for inflation each year thereafter, until you have finished your five-year stretch. Then for year six, start at the beginning of the process again (but for a total retirement that's five years shorter). In other words . . .

5. Every five years, start again. At the beginning of each five-year period, repeat the process all over again. In our illustration, you'll now be planning a 30-year retirement instead of a 35-year retirement, since you've made it through the initial five years. You'll move to the next square on the withdrawal board in Figure 8.1, which in this case (on the 99 percent safe-withdrawal track for a 30-year retirement) is 5.3 percent. Multiply 5.3 percent by the amount of money remaining in your growth portfolio, and that's the amount you'd withdraw starting year six. It most cases, this will be more than you took out for year five, but not necessarily—it might even be lower, especially if inflation has been high or the stock market has been low. Either way, this is your new base salary. For years seven through ten, you'll adjust that base amount by the rate of inflation, as we described in Step 4.

At the beginning of the next (third) five-year period, your new salary will jump to 5.6 percent times the total value of your couch potato portfolio at that point (25-year retirement, one percent risk level), so just repeat Steps 3 through 5 with this new percentage . . . and so on, changing your withdrawal rates every five years according to Figure 8.1, and adjusting every intervening year by the rate of inflation.

When you only have ten years left, we strongly suggest that you switch to the 100 percent safe-withdrawal rate going forward, which is 8.6 percent. Then continue to adjust for inflation every year thereafter.

We hasten to point out that there is no guarantee here. Our analysis may have worked swimmingly for 25,000 simulations, but that's not to say that number 25,001 won't come along and waylay us. This possibility highlights a huge truth about retirement planning: *If you want a guarantee, buy a toaster.*

This piece of wisdom holds true even if your financial planner has given you a 20-page printout with full-color charts and graphs. It always pays to watch your portfolio closely during early retirement. If a bear market hits and you're down 10 percent, tighten your belt and go to the 4 percent safe-withdrawal level.

We've included a worksheet so that you can play along at home.

Retirement Withdrawal Worksheet

Step One: Longevity Risk

1. Decide whether you want to plan for a 99% or a 95%   _____

maximum life span (see Table 3.2 on p. 63). Subtract your

retirement age from this outside figure to see how long a

retirement you're planning.

Step Two: Investment Risk

2. Decide whether you want to plan for 100%, 99%, or
95% probability of portfolio success.

Step Three: Withdrawal Rate

3. Enter the value of your couch potato portfolio: _____

4. Go to Figure 7.1 and look up your recommended   _____

portfolio withdrawal rate.

5. Multiply Line 3 by the percentage in Line 4.   _____

Withdraw this amount of money from your couch potato

portfolio at the beginning of your first year of retirement.

134

Step Four: Withdraw the Money

6. Are stocks overvalued (Y/N)?   _____

See **www.yesyoucantimethemarket.com.**

If stocks are overvalued, sell 75% stocks/25% bonds.

If stocks are undervalued, sell 25% stocks/75% bonds.

Step Four: Annual Inflation Adjustments

7. Look up the annual rate of inflation for the past year.   _____

8. Multiple Line 5 times Line 7.   _____

9. Add Line 8 to Line 5.   _____

10. Withdraw the amount in line 9 at the beginning of your

your next year of retirement.

11. Line 9 becomes the new Line 5.

Step Five: Every Five Years

12. Go back to Step 1.

Market Timing Your Withdrawals

Remember how great everyone said dollar cost averaging was, back in the days when you were saving for retirement? How the mutual fund companies cheered you on as you slung money into their stock-and-bond funds month after month, year after year, no matter what the market's price? Upon reflection, there was something a tad self-serving about these pats on the back they gave you.

Since they collect their fees based on total assets under management, nothing delights them more than the transfer of monies from you to them. When the process is put on autopilot, with a treadmill of withdrawals going from your paycheck or savings account into their coffers, it makes them happiest of all. Who among us doesn't love the feeling of money effortlessly flowing our way?

Best of all, they had a theory called *dollar cost averaging* to buttress their advice. It went like this: The market fluctuates. By deploying the same amount of money into the market each time on a fixed schedule, by definition you're buying more shares when prices are cheaper and fewer shares when prices are high. This lower cost basis makes for a bigger profit in the end, the theory says.

In retirement, unfortunately, when you're spending rather than saving, this engine gets thrown into reverse. It's called *negative* dollar cost averaging: Now in order to maintain a constant income, you have to sell more shares when prices are low, and fewer shares when prices are high. This means that *any advantage that dollar cost averaging conferred on the accumulation side is directly taken away on the distribution side.* Like Sisyphus, you'll watch helplessly as the boulder rolls down the hill.

To avoid this tragedy, we recommend that you use market timing. If stocks are overvalued (go to **www.stein-demuth.com** to find out), draw from the stock portion of your portfolio for your annual allowance. If they're undervalued, then hang on to them and sell from the bond side instead.

To illustrate this, imagine that two new retirees get into a time machine. One is a negative dollar cost averager, while the other grabs a copy of your authors' *Yes, You Can Time the Market!* before beginning his journey back to January 1, 1976.

135

Both of them set up $24,000 couch potato accounts the moment they arrive, with 50 percent of their money in the total stock market fund and 50 percent in the total bond market fund; neither pays taxes, fees, or commissions along the way. Furthermore, each decides to withdraw $100 in 1976 dollars at the beginning of every month to provide for living expenses, adjusting this amount every month by inflation.

The negative dollar cost averager sells an inflation-adjusted $50 from his stock position and $50 from his bond position on the first day of every month. Furthermore, on the first day of each year, he rebalances his accounts back to their 50-50 stock/bond allocation. By September 1, 2004 (the last quarter for which data is available as we go to press), his net worth has risen from $24,000 to $148,740, even after all withdrawals because this period was a favorable one for investors.

The reader of *Yes, You Can Time the Market!* does things differently. He sees the wisdom of evaluating the stock market before selling and determines to unload his stocks only if they appear to be overvalued by the fundamental criteria laid out in our book. If any of the measures say that stocks are undervalued, he sells $100 worth of bonds; but if stocks seemed expensive across the board, he sells $100 worth of stocks instead, adjusting this amount by inflation monthly. Furthermore, he never rebalances his account. By September 1, 2004, his initial $24,000 account—after pulling out the exact same amount of money as his negative dollar cost averaging pal—has grown to $234,134. That's 57 percent more money than his friend has.

Figure 8.3 shows the progress of these two investors' portfolios over the entire period.

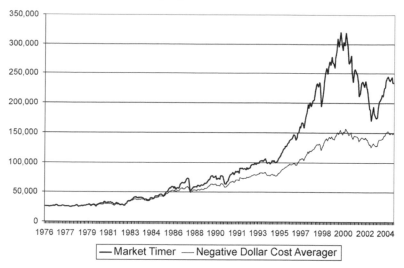

Figure 8.3: Market Timing vs. Negative Dollar
Cost Averaging Portfolio Withdrawals

Market Timer — Negative Dollar Cost Averager

Let us hasten to add that the years 1976 to 2004 present you with one possible set of investment returns, and we don't know what will happen from 2005 to 2033. In other words, this absolutely does *not* mean that if you decide to follow this method, you'll be able to take out 57 percent more money than otherwise and still be safe. It's only to suggest that market timing might confer an unknown margin of advantage over negative dollar cost averaging going forward.

We feel comfortable recommending that investors who have read our book on the subject (*Yes, You Can Time the Market!*) and understand this philosophy check our Website before making their withdrawals. If stocks appear underpriced, split the withdrawal, selling 25 percent stocks and 75 percent bonds. If stocks appear overpriced, however, do the reverse: Sell 75 percent from the stock side and 25 percent from the bond side. We think that this is an antidote to the certain damage done by negative dollar cost averaging.

The Logic of Retirement Withdrawals

Your income will vary during retirement, and we hope that this doesn't present undue hardship. Unless you had a civil-service job, you may have noticed that your income also varied from year to year before you quit working. Like most people, you probably spent more during the good times, but then cut back when you needed to—and that's what to expect when you follow our method for your later years. If you prefer to take out the same fixed amount every year during retirement, start by withdrawing 4 percent in year one and just adjust this amount by inflation thereafter.

Because you're most vulnerable to market downturns during early retirement, we recommend that you rebalance your couch potato portfolio annually for the first five years. The easiest way to do this is by drawing it down in such a way that after you take your paycheck they're once again in balance. After you've passed the first five years, rebalance when they get out of alignment by more than 10 percent—past 60/40 or 40/60.

If you've diversified part of your nest egg into an income portfolio (as discussed in the last chapter), you may want to adjust that account every five years so that its yield keeps in lockstep with the withdrawal rate of your couch potato portfolio.

However, if the couch potato portfolio has grown significantly (and considering how the withdrawal rates rise steeply in late retirement), this adjustment could become difficult or impossible without taking undue risk on the income side, depending on the interest rate environment at the time. You don't want to jump into leveraged junk bonds just to match the couch potato account's 8.6 percent withdrawal rate at that point. Use common sense.

We sincerely hope and pray that these withdrawal rates will allow you to maintain your standard of living. However, if you don't have enough savings, they may not be enough.

Then you have to go to Plan B. . . .

■ ■ ■

PART III

IF EVERYTHING YOU HAVE ISN'T ENOUGH

If you can't squeeze enough income from your financial assets to support you through the retirement of your dreams, rest assured that you have plenty of company. The obvious frontline answer is to work longer, or to work part-time through early retirement until your portfolio and Social Security can pick up the slack.

As a temporary stopgap, you might have some hidden assets lying around the house that you could sell. Still, that 1989 collection of porcelain thimbles featuring the official state birds of all 50 states may not fetch as much on eBay as you hope it will. And most individuals who don't have big stock portfolios also don't have crates full of priceless Etruscan artifacts to auction off.

Not every American life is a Horatio Alger success story—far from it. Some people devote their lives to the arts, public service, or other careers that don't leave them with investment-banker-sized portfolios. Some get divorced or have health issues or other personal setbacks. You might start a new business, putting your heart and soul into it, and it just doesn't work out. Or maybe you invest your hard-earned money in something that can't fail, and then it fails. Maybe you've simply had a string of bad luck or life dealt you a bad hand. This happens all the time.

There are three measures you can take, however, to get you through. Individually, or in some combination, they just might be enough. Each has its drawbacks, so these aren't steps to be taken lightly. But that said, they can make a tremendous difference to your quality of life in retirement.

They are: putting your assets into immediate annuities, relocating to an area with a lower cost of living, and taking out a reverse mortgage. We'll look at them one by one.

■ ■ ■

CHAPTER 9

Immediate Annuities

With the birth of tax-deferred savings accounts and tax-efficient index funds over the past decades, the demand for traditional *deferred* annuities (where you gave an insurance company money to invest tax-deferred for eventual distribution back to you at some later point) has declined significantly in recent years. Your authors discussed the merits of deferred annuities in *Yes, You Can Be a Successful Income Investor!,* so we won't go into them here.

However, with the coming baby-boom retirement crisis, the need for *immediate* annuities (where you give the insurance company a check and the payout begins immediately—and lasts for the rest of your life) will skyrocket.

Why is this? When corporations kicked their employees out of defined-benefit pension plans, in effect *every employee had to fend for him- or herself, planning for the longest possible retirement he or she might face, even though by definition half of them would experience below-average life spans.*

Professionally managed pension plans had the tremendous advantage of being able to allocate this longevity risk rationally: They used the funds from those who died early to pay for the extended retirements of those who were long-lived. The switch to "every man for himself" dramatically increases the need for you to save enough money to shepherd yourself through a superannuated retirement. This is no small difference.

A 65-year-old has an *average* life expectancy of 18.4 more years, but a *maximum* life expectancy of more than 40.2 additional years. As a cautious self-funded retiree, this means that you'll have to stretch your life's savings over at least an additional 21.8 years just to be safe.

This has enormous implications for how much you can withdraw from your portfolio every year. For example, at a 100 percent safety level, you can take out 22 percent less money initially if you have to plan for a 40-year (maximum life span) retirement instead of a 20-year (average life span) one. This has been the biggest cost of the change-over from defined-benefit to defined-contribution plans, and it hasn't even been generally recognized yet.

But buy an immediate fixed annuity, and presto—you've rejoined the retirement pool! The same nest egg only has to support you about half as long, on average. The immediate annuity, by compressing its payout to your projected actuarial life span (instead of the maximum), gives you a much higher payout.

Additionally, these immediate annuities—both fixed and variable—consume all of your principal. If you tap your nest egg yourself, whatever is left in your estate passes to your heirs. The immediate annuity, in contrast, aims to distribute all of your principal back to you in its periodic payouts. Because each paycheck contains both interest and principal, your monthly cash flow should be higher than if you were living off of the interest alone.

Furthermore, the payments will never stop as long as you (or you and your spouse, depending on the policy) are alive. You won't outlive your savings—*you'll never run out of money.*

Needless to say, with these tremendous pluses, baby boomers will be lined up around the block to buy immediate annuities.

The Single-Premium Immediate Fixed Annuity: Benefits and Risks

A single-premium immediate fixed annuity is a financial instrument whereby, in exchange for a lump sum, an insurance company offers you a steady stream of fixed payments extending over your lifetime (or if you prefer, over you and your partner's lifetime). In exchange for your one large up-front investment, they'll cut a distribution check back to you for a fixed dollar amount every month (or quarter, or year, as you prefer) for the rest of your life. No matter how much the markets go up or down in the interim, and no matter how long you live, the insurance company promises to keep the payments coming.

Because the company computes its payout based on its actuarial estimate of your life span, it doesn't have to assume that everyone will live to be 100. Even if you live to 105 and the insurance company loses money on you, they'll make it up on someone else who dies at a younger age. It's unlikely that they'll be far wrong in aggregate, as they allow for a comfortable margin of error when pricing the policy in the first place.

If you're married or in a committed relationship, you'll certainly want to get a "joint and survivor" policy that allows payments to continue to your surviving partner, should you predecease him or her. Some people are concerned that they'll mail in their check to buy an annuity and then get hit by a bus on the way back from the post office, effectively letting the insurance company walk away with all of their money (but in reality transferring it to some guy or gal at the other end of the actuarial scale who lives to be 105). For this reason, insurance companies will sell you a policy with payments that continue for a fixed period—5 years, 10 years, whatever—so that your heirs can benefit no matter what happens to you. Still other policies will pay your spouse at least up to the actuarial prediction of your death date, even if you pass on before you reach that age. These benefits are built into the price, however, and translate directly into a lower payout today.

Inflation

Fixed annuities aren't risk-free investments: The main danger they're subject to is inflation. To see how much of a factor this can be, consult Figure 9.1 (page 144), which shows how inflation eroded the value of $1,000 at the beginning of the last century. Pick any 30- or 40-year period you like and imagine what inflation could do to your fixed annuity—the one that you paid for up front using expensive, pre-inflation dollars. The purchasing power of the check that you receive later in life could easily be half of what it was when you bought the policy.

Figure 9.1: $1,000 After Inflation, 1901–2001

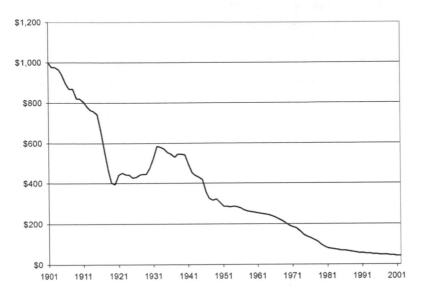

On the other hand, getting more money earlier in retirement prob-ably corresponds to your spending needs, giving you more when you really want it. But a quick upsurge in inflation shortly after purchas-ing the annuity would still have a damaging effect on the total value of the future payments you receive, and with runaway inflation, the investment would become worthless. For fixed annuity holders, the less inflation, the better—and if it must happen, the later the better.

Although you can purchase fixed annuities with an annual step-up (that is, a yearly increase) to help against the threat of a devalued currency, you'll pay extra for this feature in the form of a significantly lower initial payment. Buying this degree of inflation protection undoes some of the front-loaded income benefit that the fixed annuity would otherwise provide. This is a judgment call, based on how much the insurance company is going to charge you (in the form of a reduced initial payout). Table 9.1 shows how much an annual step-up of vary-ing amounts reduces the initial payout for a 65-year-old male buying a $100,000 policy, as of this writing. These amounts will undoubtedly be different by the time you read this, but they should give you a general idea of what to expect.

Table 9.1: Sample Costs of Annual Step-Up in a Fixed Annuity	
Annual Payout Step-Up	**Initial Annual Payout**
0%	$7,738
1%	$7,056
2%	$6,403
3%	$5,780
4%	$5,189
5%	$4,632

Remember that most policies with a step-up option don't tie themselves to the Consumer Price Index, but simply include fixed increases. If the United States experiences severe inflation and it takes a basket of dollars to buy a loaf of bread, a 3 percent annual step-up isn't going to do you much good.

As we go to press, Vanguard has begun offering an immediate fixed annuity with a built-in inflation adjustment (capped at 10 percent per year). For our 65-year-old male, selecting this option drops his annual payout by 28 percent.

Business Risk

If you buy a fixed annuity from an insurance company that goes bankrupt, you're out of luck. Your funds are commingled with theirs. Fortunately, there are rating agencies whose job it is to keep an eye on these companies, and you should only buy an annuity from one that has high marks from the likes of Standard & Poor's, Fitch, Moody's, or A. M. Best—even if you're promised a better rate by Joe's Annuity & Body Shop around the corner. Sticking with a highly rated firm will provide a measure of reassurance.

Remember that even with a famous name and a high credit rating, the actuarial tables may not anticipate some revolutionary advance in medicine that dramatically impacts longevity (such as a cure for cancer or heart disease). Were something like this to occur, even a formidable insurer could be in jeopardy. On the other hand, insurance companies did underestimate longevity in the policies they wrote in the 1930s (with all the revolutions in medicine that have occurred since), and they're still standing. These corporations tend to pocket enough money to stay afloat.

Buying a Fixed Annuity

You can generally avoid paying a salesman's commission for an immediate fixed annuity since you can purchase one directly, without the middleman, from exactly the kind of low-expense, high-reputation company that you'll want to deal with. Everything distills down to how big a payment they'll give you for your lump sum—that one figure says it all and makes it easy to compare policies. Get quotes from several providers, always making sure to compare like to like when weighing various outcomes. Our short shopping list includes getting quotations from:

- Berkshire Hathaway: **www.brkdirect.com**
- TIAA-CREF: **www.tiaa-cref.com**
- USAA: **www.usaa.com** (for veterans)
- Vanguard: **www.vanguard.com**
- Fidelity: **www.fidelity.com**

Be aware that quotes can vary widely from company to company, and even from week to week, so shop around.

Time to Buy

Whether you consider yourself to be a market timer or not, buying an immediate fixed annuity is a supreme bet on market timing, because the decisive factor underlying the quote you get will be the then-current long-term interest rate. An insurance company can't promise more than the market will bear.

If you buy when interest rates are high, and then they regress downward, you'll congratulate yourself for having made a shrewd investment. Imagine the happiness of people who locked in an annuity in 1981, when the long bond was paying more than 16 percent, only to watch interest rates fall to 4 percent today. Now the risk is just the opposite: What happens if you lock in at 4 percent and rates shoot up to 16 percent? In that case, a passbook savings account would pay you more than a fixed annuity, and you would feel like a chump for having bought one.

In *Yes, You Can Time the Market!,* we noted that those who bought government bonds during the 20th century did much better by acquiring them when interest rates were above their long-term moving averages. Figure 9.2 shows how 10-year-bond yield has varied over the past century, compared with its own 15-year moving average.

Figure 9.2: Yield on 10-Year Government Bond, 1901–2001

This counsel about buying bonds when rates are high also applies to purchasers of fixed annuities. Just as you're happier locking in your mortgage when interest rates are low, you're likely to be pleased to secure a fixed annuity when they're high. There's one important difference, though: When you buy a mortgage, you can always refinance if rates drop. Once you buy an annuity, however, you're stuck with it—that principal is gone.

Of course, it's possible that we're about to undergo decades of deflation, in which case (however unlikely) buying a fixed annuity would prove a shrewd investment. By the same token, even when rates are high by historical standards, there's no guarantee that they won't rocket even higher tomorrow, leaving your fixed annuity in tatters.

When buying a fixed annuity, it's generally best to do so when rates are high. How can you tell if they're high or low? Just go to our Website, **www.stein-demuth.com**. If rates appear to be low and you're impatient to get started anyway, the alternative is to dollar-cost average your way into the fixed-annuity pool: Buy a small fixed annuity this year, another one next year, and a third the year after that. This way, you'll diversify over time and distribute the risk somewhat.

Opportunity Cost

The $100,000 you spend on an annuity today has an invisible cost of close to a half-million (inflation-adjusted) dollars for your heirs 20 years from now. At least, that's how much it might have been worth had you invested it in the couch potato portfolio, never touched it, and earned historical rates of return. Because the annuity digests your entire payment and then returns it to you in tidy, spendable packets, unless you painstakingly save the principal payment from every check you receive (in which case, why did you buy the annuity in the first place?), the estate that you bequeath to your heirs will be reduced by the size of the original annuity payment, plus whatever returns you could have gotten on it over the remainder of your lifetime.

While you can purchase an annuity with an ongoing benefit that extends five or ten years after your death, this will significantly reduce the size of your periodic check, thus defeating a major part of the annuity's purpose. It will also constitute a taxable event for your heirs, who will be getting paid with inflated dollars in any case. At least with other capital gains (such as those from the couch potato portfolio), there's an increase in the cost basis as a consolation prize for paying the estate tax. So if you want to bequeath money, do it directly, not by buying an extended-life annuity. (But do include your spouse in the annuity, which is known as *joint survivorship*.)

Living (Almost) Forever

Longevity is a final point to consider before purchasing a fixed annuity. Many people are interested in annuities because of the promise of a lifetime stream of income—that is, the money they'll get later. We're looking at the fixed annuity because of what it can do for you today: maximizing your income stream in early retirement.

If you survive to be 105, inflation will probably have reduced the value of your payout by at least half. Relying on this as your primary source of income might not be enough (but still would be better than nothing). So if you're banking on the fixed annuity to subsidize your twilight years, buy one with a modest annual step-up in payments and cross your fingers that we don't have runaway inflation. For income later, we need to look at the fixed annuity's counterpart. . . .

The Single-Premium Immediate Variable Annuity

A single-premium immediate *variable* annuity is fundamentally a different animal from its fixed cousin. With this investment, you cut a check to the insurance company, which then takes your money and invests it in the stock and/or bond markets, typically under your direction, allowing you to choose from a menu of mutual-fund offerings. An initial payout rate is assigned, based primarily on the insurer's estimate of your longevity.

Thereafter, the periodic payment that you receive varies with the performance of your underlying portfolio of mutual funds. No matter how long you (or you and your spouse) live, the insurance underwriter will send you monthly (or quarterly, or annual) checks. If the markets prosper, the checks will increase over time; and if the market shrivels, so will your payout.

Here's the tricky part: You don't own the underlying portfolio of securities per se, but rather you're using them to try to beat the annuity's "assumed investment return" (AIR) rate. This is the rate that their initial payout is based upon (along with their estimate of your longevity). If your investments beat this AIR rate, the payout grows over time; but if they don't do as well, your payout goes down with them.

The annuity providers typically allow you to make tax-free reallocations between mutual funds, but being hinged to the under-lying markets, this means that yes, your payout really can go down. Because these annuities don't give you the actual return of your invest-ments, but instead one that's linked to the AIR, they're extremely difficult to analyze. Typically, the insurance company will send you an "illustration" that shows one scenario for how the payout might proceed. Study this closely, and consider carefully how alternate paths might affect that regular check that you'll be counting on. Here are some of the risks to factor in.

Inflation

While the fixed annuity will predictably decline in purchasing power due to inflation, the variable annuity should keep up with ordi-nary rates of inflation over long periods of time. But the value of the underlying stock portfolio could plummet if serious inflation hits, as happened in the 1970s. One low-expense provider, TIAA-CREF, allows you the option of investing your money in Treasury Inflation-Protected Securities, which is an excellent idea. Vanguard also offers this choice, at least for tax-deferred accounts.

Business Risk

There's nothing close to the same degree of individual-business risk in this case as there is with a fixed annuity, since your funds are never commingled with those of the insurance company. Even if it goes bankrupt, your investment will theoretically still be safe, and you can still transfer your annuity to another company to manage.

Living (Almost) Forever

Your nest egg should grow over the long run, providing you with increasing income in your old age. Similarly, the longer you live, the bigger your underlying stock portfolio can grow. In that respect, the variable annuity is a nice complement to the fixed annuity, which (due to inflation) has a probable front-loaded benefit.

Of course, if we're on the verge of a 30-year bear market, your income will decline. But the odds are very good that an immediate variable annuity will grow and provide you with an increasing stream of income just when you need it to take up the slack from the immediate-fixed annuity that's declining in purchasing power due to inflation.

One of your authors, Ben Stein, saw this happen for his parents, who grew well-to-do using variable annuities. This is why Ben has become the spokesman for the National Retirement Planning Coalition, one of whose members is the National Association for Variable Annuities.

Buying a Variable Annuity

Stock brokers and insurance agents will be able to show you their lineup of these products, and it's worthwhile to compare their quotes with immediate variable annuities bought directly from mutual fund sponsors themselves. Begin by taking a look at these vendors:

- TIAA-CREF: **www.tiaa-cref.com**
- Vanguard: **www.vanguard.com**
- T. Rowe Price: **www.troweprice.com**
- Fidelity: **www.fidelity.com**

Further Considerations for Both
Fixed and Variable Immediate Annuities

Despite their differences, there are still many common issues that bridge both types of immediate annuities. We'll conclude this chapter by examining these and then providing you with an example of one way to allocate funds in these investments.

Access to Principal

There's little to no access to principal with either a fixed or variable option. For a price, some companies will let you cash out a portion of your annuity later—but be sure to read all the details. The fine print is everything here, and there's lots of it. Read it, study it, and understand it.

The commitment that you make with annuities can be a good thing, if you otherwise might be tempted to overspend. At the same time, it points to the need for keeping a cash-reserve fund, since you'll no longer have your nest egg to draw upon if some emergency arises.

Your Estate

The best use of an immediate annuity is to convert a lump sum into the fattest income stream that you can get. This means translating your savings into present consumption, and not buying a policy with special provisions to continue payments to your heirs (other than your spouse) after your death. The money that you put into both fixed- and variable-immediate annuities will be gone from your estate.

Although you might find a policy that lets you continue payments past your death to benefit your heirs, this translates into a lower payout to you during your lifetime. If you can get by on this smaller amount, we think the better strategy is to simply put enough of your assets into an annuity to secure this level of income *without* recourse to the death benefit. Withhold the rest of your nest egg, and invest this leftover money in the couch potato portfolio instead. Let your heirs inherit that account instead.

Taxes

If you purchase the annuity with after-tax dollars, a sizable portion of each payment back to you will consist of a return of principal, and you won't have to pay federal income tax on it (at least until the entire amount that you paid for the annuity is returned to you). The interest will be taxable as ordinary income. These tax implications are worth pausing over.

If you're selling stocks and bonds in a taxable account in order to buy the annuity, you'll have to pay capital gains taxes on the proceeds before going to the insurance company. Also, you'll potentially be shifting more of your income to a higher tax basis, depending on your future tax bracket. But if you keep the money in stocks and bonds, you might pay a top tax rate of 15 percent on the dividends and the capital gains.

If you're still in a high tax tier after retirement, this needs to be weighed in the balance, but if your marginal tax rate is low, it may not make much difference. If you roll over your tax-deferred retirement accounts into a fixed annuity, all the proceeds will be taxable as income, so this will be tax-neutral.

For these reasons, it's a very good idea to run the idea of purchasing an annuity past your accountant before taking action—especially since the U.S. tax code is a moving target and may change significantly between the time we're writing this and the time you're ready to buy. For example, annuities were left behind by the Job & Growth Tax Relief Reconciliation Act of 2003. Will they be given better tax treatment in the future? Only your congressional representatives know.

See IRS Publication 939, General Rule for Pensions and Annuities, for the details on how to calculate taxes due on annuity payments. Believe it or not, some states charge a tax on your annuity premium. This is a low blow indeed. Go to **www.annuity.com/main/premtax. cfm** to find out if you live in one of them.

How Much to Allocate?

Even if you have no bequest motives, you'll still want to keep a significant amount of money in a cash-reserve account in case of emergencies. After that, the more that you put into an annuity, the higher your payments will be, with the least amount of risk. On the other hand, you need to compare what your annuity payout will be versus what you might get by escalating the risk in your couch potato and income portfolios. If these latter accounts by themselves can meet your needs, then you have no need to look to annuities (with their attendant fees and dramatic impact on your estate). If you're on the fence, you might be able to get by only sinking a portion of your assets into annuities and keeping the rest to grow independently.

Dividing Between Fixed and Variable Annuities

In a paper written for Ibbotson Associates, analyst Peng Chen and Professor Moshe Milevsky conclude that the best allocation between fixed and variable annuities is essentially the same as it is for non-annuitized assets. Taking the couch potato portfolio as your model, this might lead you to put half your money in a fixed annuity (as you did with the total bond market) and half in a variable annuity (as with the total stock market). However, there are some important respects in which the couch potato portfolio is different from going the fixed-plus-variable-annuity route.

While a fixed annuity has a constant, unvarying return, the yield of the total bond market fluctuates from month to month. It can be expected to grow over time (unlike the annuity), and it's not subject to the ravages of inflation to the same degree.

Because of this, while the couch potato portfolio is 50 percent stocks and 50 percent bonds, we recommend that retirees who choose annuities for their assets use a different ratio: Put 65 percent in a variable annuity (invested mostly in stocks) and 35 percent in a fixed annuity. This should pay enough to supplement early retirement with extra income from the fixed side, while giving time for the stock portfolio in the variable annuity to grow and later make up for the shrinking purchasing power of the fixed annuity payout (due to inflation).

Medical Underwriting

One more thought: Most immediate annuities are determined by a simple look at actuarial mortality tables, without recourse to your personal medical history (no doctor visit required). However, people who choose annuities tend to be a long-lived bunch, so you'll be grouped with this especially healthy lot (not the general population) for determining your monthly payment. Since the insurance company suspects that you're going to be around longer than average, your monthly payout will be a bit smaller that you might expect.

If you have some health issue that might make you less long-lived than others folks who apply for annuities, you can request a quote from a company that offers medical underwriting. These include Fidelity & Guaranty (**note:** this is a different company from Fidelity Investments Life Insurance), Genworth Financial, and Lincoln Benefit Life. They may give you a better deal.

Let's look at a specific example to bring all these factors into focus.

Immediate Annuities—an Illustration

Let's assume that you are a single 70-year-old female with $100,000 to annuitize, and you choose to do business with Vanguard. The quotes that we obtained are valid today but undoubtedly will be different by the time you read this. You can punch in your own situation by going to **http://flagship.vanguard.com/VGApp/hnw/FundsAnnuity**.

Following our recipe of putting 35 percent in a fixed annuity and 65 percent in a variable annuity, she first places $35,000 of her money into Vanguard's fixed-annuity option. Today, that gives her $3,020 per year income for life. This will be impacted by inflation, so the payout probably will be worth more today than it will later on.

Next, she places $65,000 into a variable annuity. With an assumed-investment return of 3.5 percent, this will bring in an initial $5,182 per year. (Remember: The AIR is a formula that the insurance company uses to set your initial payout rate. Thereafter, your payments go up if your returns are above this rate, and they go down if your returns fall below it.)

Combined with her fixed annuity, this makes her check from Vanguard in year one come to $8,202—a tidy sum to add to her Social Security benefits. This is an 8.2 percent yield on her money, and more than she would have received using any of our couch potato or diversified income strategies.

With the variable annuity, she still has to make some decisions about which funds to invest her money in. Using the offerings Vanguard provides, we recommend that she choose the ones in Table 9.2.

Table 9.2: Variable Annuity Allocations

Vanguard Portfolios:	Allocation
Total Stock Market	40%
Total International Index	30%
Total Bond Market*	20%
REIT Index	10%

Substitute inflation-indexed bonds if using pre-tax dollars.

Note that we haven't duplicated the couch potato portfolio in this account. We know exactly which funds Vanguard offers and have made a diversified, low-expense selection of index offerings, mindful that 35 percent of her income is locked into the fixed annuity. Based on the historical performance of these asset classes, most years (but by no means every year) her income should rise.

If she'd bought her variable annuity from TIAA-CREF (historically the lowest-cost provider), we would have recommended that she allocate her variable-annuity portfolio as shown in Table 9.3.

Table 9.3: Variable Annuity Allocations

TIAA-CREF Portfolios:	Allocation
Stock Index	30%
International Equity	20%
TIPS	20%
Large Cap Value	10%
Small Cap Equity	10%
Real Estate Security	10%

As with the Vanguard funds, the TIAA-CREF portfolio has a good chance of supporting an increased payout most years.

Fidelity Investments, another good company, has of late increased its entire slate of offerings to retirees, and also offers fixed- and variable-immediate annuities. As an illustration, we might recommend that she put 35 percent of her $100,000 into Fidelity's guaranteed (that is, fixed) annuity and distribute the remaining 65 percent into their variable annuity offerings, choosing the funds in Table 9.4.

Table 9.4: Variable Annuity Allocations	
Fidelity Portfolios:	**Allocation**
Fidelity VIP Index 500	40%
Morgan Stanley Int'l. Magnum	30%
Fidelity VIP Value Strategies	10%
Fidelity VIP Health Care	10%
Fidelity VIP Real Estate	10%

All these allocations should be considered suggestive rather than definitive.

In summary, given the largely irreversible nature of the decision to annuitize your savings, and its vast importance to your financial future, make sure that the annuity's provisions are as clear to you as the rules for tic-tac-toe before you sign away your nest egg. As people clamor to convert their savings into cash for life, the market for immediate annuities will expand dramatically from the niche it occupies today. With this expansion should come greater transparency, better economies of scale, and increased options to personalize a plan to fit your income needs. These investments will be the salvation of many baby boomers and Gen Xers.

■ ■ ■

CHAPTER 10

Relocate

If you're retired and want to make your money go further, you can move to an area with a lower cost of living. We didn't have you include the value of your home in your retirement-savings program earlier, but you probably have a pretty good idea of what your residence is worth. By selling it and downsizing, the difference in price between your current house and the new one can go straight into your savings. If you choose an area with a lower overall cost of living, your expenses going forward will decrease as well.

But whether you're thinking of relocating to a beach house in Maui or to the sofa in your daughter's living room, you're going to have to make some psychological adjustments in order to get used to the new situation. It usually takes several years for even the most socially adaptable among us to get a new town "wired"—don't underestimate the wear and tear involved. No matter what may be said about your current residence, it's the devil you know. Relocating will involve trading this for the devil you don't know (or, at least, that you don't know as well).

Moving won't be painless either. There will be the transition expenses of investigating a new place to live, fixing up and selling your current home, paying the Realtors and the movers, finding that your prized crystal egg was scratched en route, discovering that the new roof leaks, learning that the place next door is a halfway house for sex offenders, and so on. This isn't a process for the faint of heart.

The key factor driving everything is the profit that you can wrest from the difference between the cost of living where you reside at present and that of your retirement destination. If you own a large penthouse on the Upper East Side of Manhattan, with commanding views of Central Park, you'll have a lot of choices for downward mobility. But if you currently live in the back of a horse trailer in Plutonium Springs, Wyoming, the same lifestyle options just won't be available, because any place you can move will be at least as expensive as where you're already living.

By all means go to the library and check out a stack of books on great, cheap places to retire—just be aware that they're full of lies. With thousands of boomers finishing their careers every day, all the nice places will be overrun by retiring "dumpies" (destitute unprepared mature persons, or former yuppies) before you get there. Since prices are set by supply and demand, housing costs in today's tony retirement towns may be out of reach when you arrive—unless you happen to be in the first wave to hit the shore.

Fortunately, you can get a quick read from the Internet on what to expect in terms of sticker shock. Look up Sperling's Best Places (**www. bestplaces.net**), click on "Cost of Living," and you'll get an instant answer on what it costs to live in your present burg versus the retirement haven that you've got your eye on. If you don't see a substantial difference (more than 10 percent), there's probably no point in moving, unless you have some other motivating factor.

But even on Websites such as this, the housing data may be several years old, which means that it's obsolete. Since the biggest single expense that you're going to have in your new town is the cost of buying a home, you need current information. For this, punch the prospective city and state into Realtor.com (**www.realtor.com**) in order to see what you might buy in your price range today, not five years ago. Remember, the listings that you see show asking prices—homes may actually sell for less.

Obviously, you'll want to do as much research as you can from your home base. Talk to anyone you know who's relocated or lives in the area of interest, and milk the Internet for all it's worth. For once, chat rooms really might have valuable information, if they contain residents talking about local life. Then, and only then, should you turn to your spouse and say, "Road trip!"

From Metropolis to Smallville

Let's look at a list of a few places that are still affordable for most people as of this writing. These communities love having retirees come to roost, because you'll pay taxes without consuming local resources the way that younger families with children do.

Fayetteville, Arkansas

Set on Beaver Lake, Fayetteville is a town of 60,000, plus some 15,000 students from the University of Arkansas. The school is key, because baby boomers will never completely retire, they'll just go to graduate school. All of the cultural and intellectual resources of a major university—classes, arts programs, athletics, lectures, and libraries—lie waiting to be plundered.

Fayetteville has a moderate climate, the beauty and recreational opportunities of the Ozark Mountains, and even historical significance (a Civil War battlefield). It seems to have everything that a senior could want, except a teaching hospital (for cutting-edge treatment) and a Starbucks (although the coffee chain will probably get there before you do). Best of all, it has a low cost of living relative to the rest of the country—especially in the all-important areas of housing and health care.

Branson, Missouri

If you love country music, look no further. There are 60 shows playing at some 30 venues in Branson—a town of 6,000. In addition to a long list of recreational activities that make it a family destination for six million tourists every summer, the Ozark mountains and surrounding lakes are there, too. It's like retiring to a theme park, swarming in the summer and quiet in the winter. The climate is reasonable and so are the prices. If your taste runs to the Guarneri Quartet, you might do better in a college town.

Ocala, Florida

Ocala is very possibly the cheapest city in the retirement destination that is Florida, and health-care costs are also well below national averages. The climate is mild, and retirees abound. An agricultural and horse-farm community set in the northern interior of the state, Ocala is within striking distance of the beaches and Orlando, which is helpful when relatives come to visit. Gainesville, a big college town, is 35 miles away.

Daytona Beach, Florida

If you must retire closer to the water, the budget-minded retiree can settle in Daytona Beach. There's more action than in some of the other Florida spots we mention: more restaurants, a big NASCAR race every year, and beaucoup tourists—especially during spring break, when the town is overrun by college kids in pursuit of adult education.

New Port Richey, Florida

Alternatively, if you want to be on the Gulf coast, the town of New Port Richey recommends itself. Its main attraction is a low cost of living (except for houses on the beach, of course) while still being within commuting distance of Clearwater (23 miles), St. Petersburg (34 miles), and Tampa (38 miles), with everything that these cities have to offer in the way of cultural amenities. Just remember that you'll need a car to get to them.

Oxford, Mississippi

The home of Ole Miss, this is a classic southern small town dripping with charm (population 11,000, with an equal number of students). Oxford makes many of the "best places to retire" lists for its combination of small-town comfort and university life, all at low cost, although there's no teaching hospital. William Faulkner lived here, and John Grisham does today. Find out more on the town's Website devoted to luring you south: **retire.oxfordms.com**.

Fairhope, Alabama

Another quaint and charming southern town, this one is on the Gulf of Mexico. Think gnarled oaks hanging with Spanish moss and sunsets on the bay. Fairhope is a town on the grow, and is struggling to preserve its character by fending off Wal-Mart and major developers. It's a 19-mile drive from Mobile, Alabama, which has the conveniences of a larger city.

Kerrville or Fredericksburg, Texas

These communities are located 24 miles apart in the Texas hill country. Kerrville has the Guadalupe River flowing through town, while the somewhat-smaller Fredericksburg celebrates its German heritage. Both are affordable and have rugged outdoor scenery and a more temperate climate (less humidity) than the towns we've mentioned in Florida, Alabama, and Mississippi. A car is a must, since major medical procedures will require a trip to San Antonio, some 65 miles away. And why not consider San Antonio itself while you're there—it also has a significantly lower-than-average cost of living.

Clayton, Georgia

This is a small (population 2,016) town in the foothills of the Blue Ridge Mountains by Lake Burton. It's beautiful, safe, and inexpensive (for now); and the climate is extremely user-friendly. For a tertiary-care medical center, you do have to go to Atlanta, some 100 miles away. Clayton is the center of life in Rabun County, however, and offers more attractions than one would expect for a town of its size.

There are plenty of other places to consider that might still be cheap, depending on your preferences: Billings, Montana; Sioux Falls, South Dakota; Toledo, Ohio; Brownsville, Texas; and Pensacola, Florida come to mind. More new ones will be discovered or invented as these fill up.

Table 10.1 summarizes some of the vital statistics about these towns, taken from Sperling's Best Places and Realtor.com. Note that the median-housing information lists *asking* prices for detached single-family homes in the area as of February 2005; sale prices are undoubtedly lower. The retiree-tax-friendliness rating is in the considered judgment of *Bloomberg Wealth Manager* magazine, and for the cost-of-living data, 100 = the U.S. average.

Table 10.1: City Statistics

	Branson, MO	Fayetteville, AR	Ocala, FL	Daytona Beach, FL	New Port Richey, FL	Oxford, MI	Fairhope, AL	Kerrville, TX	Fredericksburg, TX	Clayton, GA
Population	5,549	58,163	47,926	64,706	15,305	13,259	13,112	20,556	9,667	1,728
Median household income	$31,477	$30,466	$32,015	$27,723	$24,462	$22,735	$41,465	$26,429	$27,155	$23,394
Cost of Living										
Overall	97.8	98.5	91.5	90.1	93.0	87.5	92.7	92.9	91.6	93.5
Housing	105.7	111.0	73.9	77.3	71.6	78.2	87.8	87.0	83.1	89.4
Food	91.5	89.4	98.4	100.9	105.1	96.3	95.2	92.1	88.3	96.7
Transportation	99.0	94.4	105.4	90.4	103.4	92.1	94.0	96.7	96.2	90.5
Utilities	84.5	88.1	90.4	102.4	98.9	83.7	105.8	84.5	93.1	100.1
Health Care	96.8	89.0	104.7	97.3	112.5	87.6	83.9	99.0	98.7	98.0
Miscellaneous	95.7	95.5	101.1	93.8	101.9	92.8	94.8	100.7	100.7	94.8
House Median Asking Price	$170,000	$199,900	$165,000	$165,000	$217,000	$199,000	$229,000	$168,000	$254,000	$239,000
Property Tax	$11.00	$8.70	$23.10	$14.70	$17.50	$9.90	$3.80	$23.40	$23.40	$15.80
Sales Tax	6.70%	6.20%	6.35%	6.35%	6.35%	7.00%	7.45%	8.05%	8.05%	6.65%
Income Tax	6.00%	7.00%	0%	0%	0%	5.00%	5.00%	0%	0%	6.00%
Retiree Tax Friendliness	D+	B+	B+	B+	B+	A-	A+	D+	D+	B+

Unfortunately, as with all such lists, this one can become obsolete almost immediately. Many observers feel that the U.S. housing market is due for a correction, which could have a big impact on the arbitrage between what your house is worth where you live today and what houses may cost in a community where you want to relocate. There are no perfect rankings detailing the expense to live in various cities, let alone what they'll cost by the time you get there. So once you've narrowed it down to a likely candidate, the best way to find this information is to rent. Go live there for six months, preferably taking in part of the good season and part of the bad, and see whether you like it and what it really costs.

Retiring Abroad

If these U.S. locations still seem out of reach, you have the option to retire abroad. Your best bet is going to be Mexico, Costa Rica, or some other country in Central America. Canada might be attractive (with its socialized medicine), but if living in a lower-cost area of the United States is too expensive, you won't find Canada any cheaper. New Zealand and South Africa might be affordable once you get there, but coming and going from the U.S. is expensive—and you do plan to come back occasionally, don't you? Don't forget that friends and family will be visiting, too.

Central American countries such as Belize, Panama, Nicaragua, and Honduras don't have well-entrenched, sizable, permanent colonies of U.S. citizens at present—but they will. For right now, your best bet really is Costa Rica or Mexico.

We recently saw a Website proclaiming that Costa Rica is full of beautiful women who are extremely generous and giving by nature, blind to a man's age, and who consider any American male with a Social Security check to be a millionaire. We suspect that this is untrue, and it illustrates an important point: Keep your wits about you as you research. Ask yourself: *What am I being sold?* It may be tours, real estate, or some other commodity, but most of the information that's easy to get comes from people who want to make money off of you in one way or another. There's just no substitute for talking to locals (on the

Internet), then visiting, and finally renting for six months to get the feel of the place.

If your goal is to save money by retiring abroad, you have to recognize that it's easy to spend as much in Mexico or Costa Rica as you would in one of the lower-cost-of-living areas in the United States—but in the U.S. you get to keep your Medicare benefits. Remember this truth: "Live like an American—pay like an American." If you attempt to completely re-create your Upper East Side or Malibu lifestyle in a foreign country, don't expect to save a lot of money.

Let's take a closer look at each of these destinations.

Mexico

To get the lowdown on the expat scene in Mexico today, we contacted Geoffrey Katz, who publishes the highly literate *Adventures in Mexico* newsletter (**www.mexico-newsletter.com**). Geoffrey reports that thanks to ATMs, the Internet, cable TV, chain stores such as Wal-Mart and Sam's Club, cell phones, UPS, and FedEx—as well as easy air access to every major U.S. city—living in Mexico is increasingly transparent with life in the United States. People from California who were dropped into a shopping mall in Guadalajara would scarcely recognize that they'd left home (until they saw the prices in pesos), since all the stores and restaurants would be familiar name brands. Furthermore, many Mexicans speak some English and have relatives living in the U.S.

— *How much?* Most current retirees in Mexico claim that they're there for the love of the place, not just to save money. The climate is sunny; and it's possible to live with blend of modern commerce, Spanish-colonial architecture, and traditional Indian open-air markets offering fruits, vegetables, and crafts. There are beaches, good restaurants, culture, and gracious social manners.

Just as attractive, however, is this: You can live in Mexico for half of what you can in the U.S. If you retire with $200,000 in the bank and a $1,500 Social Security check every month, you'll live well. With $500,000 in assets, you'll be able to have a house in a fancy neighborhood with calla lilies and amaryllis in clay pots out front, and a nonstop travel budget. Speak Spanish fluently (one year of study, maybe start learning now?) and it's like having an extra $100,000, because you can bargain like a native instead of a tourist. Meanwhile, a $20 bill can buy dinner for two with drinks in a nice restaurant.

Not only are housing costs low—perhaps $100,000, on average—but the surprising part is how little the ongoing outlays are. This is a country that barely taxes real estate assets, subsidizes the cost of electricity, and has a climate so temperate that neither heating nor air conditioning is required. There's no home-owner's insurance, and house maintenance costs are low, since stone and tile don't tend to wear out, and workmen to repair them can be hired cheaply. The entire service economy—including in-home nursing care, language and music lessons, massages, gardening, pool maintenance, cooking, shopping, accounting, and so on—is far less expensive than in the United States. A ticket to an elegant symphony concert runs $13.

— *Location, location, location.* The first thing to do is get away from the international-tourist destinations such as Mexico City, Cuernavaca, and Cancún, which are extremely expensive. The next tier is the retirement colonies around Lake Chapala and San Miguel de Allende—a place that's experiencing a housing bubble of its own, and where $250,000 might be an entry-level price for something modest and centrally located. If you're looking for safety in numbers, you should know that the one of the largest expatriate communities is in Guadalajara.

U.S. retirees with $100,000 to $125,000 to spend on housing are finding ample choices of high-quality construction in fine neighborhoods throughout the country in Mexico's colonial cities, and in pleasant beach towns up and down the coasts. $200,000 and up gets you a pool, gardens, terraces, and views over the city. At $250,000–300,000, you can come to the table in San Miguel de Allende, find something nice with a pool and gardens at Lake Chapala, or live in a gated neighborhood in one of the colonial cities.

Rentals seem to be less readily available. Prices for good apartments begin at about $400 and go to $800+ for something with a luxury feel and a nice view, while house rentals run $500 to $1,000. Rates are similar in the Lake Chapala area, but triple these ranges for good locations in San Miguel de Allende.

The colonial cities such as Morelia, San Luis Potosí, Oaxaca, Colima, Veracruz, Mérida, Guanajuato, Zacatecas, and San Cristóbal de las Casas all offer sophistication and culture. The beach towns have less culture but more sand and water. Retirees are presently filtering into the Quintana Roo coast along the so-called Mayan Riviera below Cancún, and inland as far as Lake Bacalar. On the Pacific side, they're heading to Huatulco, Puerto Escondido, Puerto Vallarta, and Mazatlán. There are also the Pacific-coast hideaway spots of Troncones, Chacala, Barra de Potosí, Barra de Navidad/Melaque, Mazunte, Maruata, Sayulita, and San Francisco.

And if none of these sound appealing, you can always move farther south. . . .

Costa Rica

Costa Rica is reportedly home to 40,000 U.S. expats, who live there at least part-time, and it's become a trendy, upscale ecotourist destination as well. If you ever get lonely for home, just hang out at the bar at the Four Seasons and get your fill of gossip about what's going on in Bridgehampton or Marin County. Like Mexico, Costa Rica offers a you a choice between living closer to the cultural and political center of San José (with the University of Costa Rica, private medical clinics, and high-speed Internet access), located in the highly temperate central valley; or more of a "surf and turf" lifestyle in the Pacific beach towns, some developed and touristy, some not. Of course, costs can vary widely.

— *How much?* A determinedly frugal single person might live on as little as $1,000 a month, and a couple on $1,500. This means no car, renting a small place, and eating in. And if you speak Spanish, shop with the locals, and generally live as they do, it will be cheaper than in the U.S.

If you want to join the "Caja" for socialized health care, it will cost you about $800 per year—and be prepared to put up with all the inconveniences of bureaucratized medicine. The private clinics (which can include large hospitals) are where you'll want to go for anything serious; and while these are expensive, they'll still charge far less than their counterparts in the United States. There are respectable private nursing homes where you might stay for $1,000 per month. Adding around-the-clock private care might add another $1,200 to this figure, but that's still substantially less than what a similar arrangement would cost back home.

— *Location, location, location.* The American ambassador lives in the San José suburb of Escazú, an expensive town teeming with expats. Better deals will be found in places a bit farther afield such as Santa Ana, Alajuela, Grecia, Cartago, and Sarchí. To get used to the place, you might consider a more upscale rental in Escazú to get your bearings, and then venture out as you discover your likes and dislikes. While you can easily spend a million dollars for a house here (as you also could, for example, in the Pacific beach towns of Tamarindo or Playas del Coco), an American-style home will cost at least $300,000. As you move to less fashionable surrounds, the prices might fall to less than half of this. While anyone can call him- or herself a real-estate agent and there's no multiple-listing service at present, at least there's a well-established system of property rights for residents that also extends to foreigners (Costa Rica improves on Mexico in this regard). You can browse for properties on the Web, but those listings will be the cream of the crop—and priced accordingly.

As wonderful as all of this is, there are still some disadvantages to leaving the U.S.

Drawbacks to Retiring Abroad

There are significant drawbacks to retiring abroad, and we don't want to gloss over them. One wrench in the works is the status of the U.S. dollar, which seems to be in decline for now. The advantage gained by retiring abroad can be eroded by a decline in the dollar's purchasing power, just as it can if you put your savings into a foreign currency that undergoes a major devaluation (as the Mexican peso has experienced, for example).

When Social Security deposits your check in Banco de México, the first thing the bank does is convert your dollars to pesos at the prevailing exchange rates. When the U.S. currency is strong, you reap the benefit, but if the dollar weakens relative to the peso (or, in Costa Rica, the colón), you can get stung. This hurts retirees back in the U.S. to some extent as well, since they also wish to buy goods made abroad.

Still, even though the dollar has declined significantly against the yen and the euro of late, it hasn't gone down in relation to the currencies of Mexico and Costa Rica. In fact, in 2004, the dollar actually *appreciated* 9.5 percent relative to the colón. On the other hand, inflation in Costa Rica that year was just over 13 percent.

But there's more to consider than purchasing power in the local plaza. For instance, while Social Security will be happy to deposit your check in a foreign bank, Medicare stops at the U.S. borders. Health care may be cheaper abroad, but what are you getting? Do you really want that country doctor to perform a quadruple bypass on you? If not, you'll have to return to the U.S. for major procedures (which, in the event of an emergency, might also require an expensive evacuation). Prescription drugs might be cheaper in Costa Rica, but if you're paying out of your own pocket for a new biotech treatment, it could still cost $10,000 or more each year. In short, if you can afford it, you're going to want private health insurance. This could add at least $5,000 per year to the cost of retiring abroad.

You're also going to need to be very flexible, and this means more than just learning to use the metric system. A couple of the challenges include putting up with a "mañana" attitude for things that you want done today and extending yourself to make new friends—not to mention the substantial stress of relocation to what at first may seem like another planet, and dealing with bouts of homesickness.

If you're part of a couple, there's the additional issue of what happens when one of you dies. Will your spouse be comfortable soldiering on without you in a foreign land? And a country that's great for active seniors might be less desirable if you eventually require long-term care. These are possibilities that have to be faced, and it's a good idea to have an exit or "repatriation" strategy.

But be comforted by the fact that baby boomers are turning 50 at the rate of 10,000 each day. There will be a lot of people confronting

171

these issues, which means that a certain economy of scale will set in, bringing with it the likelihood of market-driven solutions. This means that unless you're part of the very first wave of retiring baby boomers in some undeveloped region, you won't have to be the trailblazing pioneer who ends up with arrows in his back. There will be a super-highway leading to these foreign-retirement havens.

If you've decided to relocate within the U.S., however, there's one more step that you can take: a reverse mortgage, which is the subject of our final chapter.

■ ■ ■

CHAPTER 11

Reverse Mortgages

It's estimated that between 77 and 82 percent of baby boomers own their own homes. In most cases, this is their main asset—especially now, after several years of rising prices in the housing market (which may be over by the time you read this). For the cash-strapped retiring boomer, the question naturally arises: *How do I get this money out of my house and into my wallet?* There are three ways of tapping the wealth that you currently have locked into your home. Let's take them one by one.

The first way to profit from this asset is to **sell your house outright.** After paying 6 percent in commissions (and whatever "fix-up" expenses the sale entails, plus subsequent moving expenses), a single owner who's lived in the home for two out of the past five years is entitled to a $250,000 exemption from capital gains taxes on the proceeds, and a couple can pull out $500,000 in tax-free profits. While it's nice that the government gives you this break, at the same time you need to acknowledge that the total transaction costs of selling a home and moving are steep: By the time you make any needed repairs and hire a mover, they can easily hit 10 percent.

If you go ahead with the sale, you'll end up with the cash and ask yourself, *What next?* Well, you could invest the money and rent, or you could move to an area with a lower cost of living, as we discussed in Chapter 10.

Or, you could forego selling and opt for what's behind door number two:

A second way to tap in to the value of your home is to **take out a mortgage or a home-equity line of credit.** For retirees, there's a big problem here: In order to qualify for these loans, you need to document a source of regular income—usually something beyond Social Security. If you're unemployed, there may not be sufficient income to qualify. The bank isn't going to let you borrow 80 percent of the value of your home with a promise that you'll use part of the money they give you to pay back the loan itself. Since the total cost of the loan will far exceed the amount of cash you get up front, there won't be any way for you to raise enough money to pay it back without investing in the stock market—which might turn against you. And if you're borrowing the money merely to invest it, in order to pay it back, then what was the point of borrowing in the first place?

Of course, if you do have ongoing, documentable income, you might be able to get a mortgage or line of credit. However, if you have this much of a cash flow, you probably don't need the loan in the first place. Just remember that with mortgages and lines of credit, banks want to be paid every month. This obligation will stick to you like glue until it's paid off.

This leaves choice number three—the reverse mortgage.

What Is a Reverse Mortgage?

A reverse mortgage is a loan based on your home's value, which you'll repay to the lender with the proceeds of its sale—whenever that may be. This option has several advantages. The first generation of these offerings were often outright scams, and retirees are justifiably wary as a result. As better protections have been put in place for seniors, your authors have come to like these loans a bit more than we used to.

There's no income requirement as a qualification, because you don't pay back the loan until you actually sell your home, so the problem of a bank's foreclosing on you for failing to make your payments never arises. When you finally do sell, there are guarantees in place to ensure that the total value of the loan will never exceed the amount realized from the sale—they can't tap any of your other assets to recoup their losses. This is true even if your home declines in value and becomes worth less than the total value of the loan.

The qualifications aren't onerous. For the federally insured reverse mortgage, the Home Equity Conversion Mortgage (HECM), you have to be 62 years old (so do both owners, in the case of a couple), and you have to own your residence. It can be a single-family home, a federally approved condominium, a co-op, or a two- to four-unit building. Mobile homes don't qualify, but manufactured homes might if they're set on a permanent foundation. The structure must be your principal place of residence (that is, you live there more than half of the year), and it must be paid off. What if you still have a mortgage? There's a work-around: You can use a portion of your reverse mortgage to pay it off.

How Much Can You Get?

The answer depends on a number of variables: your age, prevailing interest rates, loan costs, the value of your home, whether you're going through the federally insured program or a private lender, and when you want the money.

Here's how it works: The older you are, the more money a bank or other lender will give you today, because the future value of the loan (based on your life expectancy) is discounted back to the present over a shorter period of time. Most applicants who opt for reverse mortgages are around 75 years old.

The lower that interest rates are right now, the more you can get, because that low rate is locked in—which means that the sum you'll end up owing will be lower than if it had been subject to higher interest rates in the future. In this respect, a reverse mortgage is an attractive offering in a low-interest-rate environment.

And in terms of fees, if you go with a low-cost loan provider, there will be more money for you and less for them.

The value of your residence is another limiting factor. If a broker tells you that your home is worth a million dollars, that doesn't mean that a bank will let you borrow that much against it. The federal program has strict limits—called "203(b)" limits—capping the loan, which vary from county to county. In rural areas, you'll top out at $160,176. If you own a more expensive home in a rural area, Fannie Mae's "Home Keeper" reverse-mortgage product may give you more money, since it has one cap for the entire country (although, by the same token, it's generally not competitive elsewhere).

In cities, the amount of the HECM loan goes up to $295,319. Your town house in Manhattan is worth $6 million? That's fine, but the maximum amount of the federally sponsored loan you receive will still be $295,319. This figure is itself an outside limit—depending on your age, the top amount you can get will probably be far less.

With an expensive home, you can pull out a bigger chunk of its value by going through a private lender. If you have a million-dollar property, though, a reverse mortgage will have to be weighed against the prospect of downsizing to a more modest home in your same area or relocating to someplace with a lower cost of living, and then investing the difference. You can even take out an HECM reverse mortgage on your new, smaller house, if you choose.

The credit limits set by HECM may actually match up with many baby boomers' home equity situation. A 65-year-old couple who owns a $300,000 house in Los Angeles County (which would be a modest spread, given Southern California's current housing boom) can choose to tap in to it for $929 per month for the rest of their lives. This extra $11,148 each year will be a worthwhile supplement to Social Security, although it will be affected by inflation, meaning that it may diminish in purchasing power over time—or to look at it another way, it will likely provide the couple with more income earlier, during the more active phase of their retirement.

If they wait until age 70, however, they can take out $12,672 annually; and if they postpone making withdrawals until 75, the amount will rise to $14,664. These values come from actuarial calculations and won't be revised upward later, after the borrowing process begins. That is, once you start the monthly withdrawals, you lock in the payment you're going to get forever.

Withdrawal and Investment Options

As an alternative to monthly payments, you could withdraw the entire amount in one lump sum, which raises the question of what to do with all that cash. If you invest it in a bear market, you risk losing it—and then there will be no more reverse mortgage to fall back on. If you put it in the bank, you'll earn a lower rate of interest than the one at which either you or your estate will have to repay the loan.

You can also use the money to buy an immediate fixed annuity and possibly get a higher lifetime payout than that provided by the loan, but with one difference: The income from the annuity will be taxable, while the cash from the reverse mortgage is tax-free (after all, it's a loan).

Buying an annuity with the lump-sum proceeds from a reverse mortgage makes three people very happy: The bank who lends you the money and charges you a fee for their trouble; the insurance company selling you the annuity, whose fee is built into the size of the payout they give you every month; and Uncle Sam, who gets to tax your income.

177

The fact that the fees may be largely invisible to you and wrapped into the loan still doesn't make this a frictionless transaction. The difference in the tax status of the two sources of income would more than make up for the difference. After taxes, the reverse mortgage loan should be worth more.

The worst thing you could do with the lump sum is to spend it on present consumption. Sure, you could buy a new Aston Martin, but what then? You'd be staring at decades of potential poverty with no recourse. We mention this because most people who get a lump sum of money to pay off credit-card debt find themselves in trouble with their credit cards again 18 months later, along with having their additional *über*-loan to pay off.

Reverse mortgages give you the option of splitting the payout: taking part of it as a lump sum (to pay off your mortgage, for example) and the remainder either in the form of monthly payments or as a credit line to tap as needed. With an HECM or jumbo private loan, this credit line grows with every year you put off getting it. We think that the best use of this resource is to withdraw the money only as you need it, just as you might do with a home-equity loan that you get pre-retirement.

Fees

One great feature of reverse mortgage loans is that (unlike conventional forward mortgage loans) it's possible to make head-to-head comparisons of their total costs. All the usual characters will be standing there with their hands out to take your cash:

- An origination fee of up to $2,000, or 2 percent of the loan's value.

- *Closing costs:* A home-appraisal fee, a title search and title insurance, surveys, inspections, recording fees, taxes, a credit report, state fees, county taxes, escrow/settlement fees, document costs, and so on.

- With an HECM loan, 2 percent of the total value of the loan is charged to your balance on day one. If you die the next day, your estate is still out that much money. This charge is used to insure against the risks that your eventual payment could be greater than the future value of your home. An additional 0.5 percent on your loan's balance is added every year for the same reason. Private insurers don't guarantee your loan in this manner, but use more conservative assumptions in calculating the initial-loan amount.

- A servicing fee for administering your loan, typically $30 to $35 a month.

- And finally, the interest on the loan: With HECM, this is the one-year T-bill rate plus 1.5 percent. For the private (jumbo) mortgages, this is the 6 month LIBOR (London Interbank Offered Rate—the most widely used benchmark for short-term interest rates) plus 5 percent. This week, the difference is 4.21 percent for HECM and 7.77 for the private loan. Although this interest isn't paid until your house is sold, it shows that the HECM option will eat away at your home equity more slowly, if it otherwise provides enough to meet your needs.

With a reverse mortgage, all of these charges are built into the Total Annual Loan Cost (TALC). This is the rate that the insurer is charging you, from soup to nuts. The fact that the TALC exists allows you to shop for a reverse mortgage entirely on price. In this respect at least, reverse mortgages are consumer friendly, and it shows how senior citizens have become a protected species.

Risks

Taking out a reverse mortgage is not a risk-free transaction. If you fail to (a) make your property-tax payments, (b) maintain your home-owner's insurance, or (c) keep your house in suitable repair, the bank can foreclose to protect its investment.

The lender can also step in if the home is no longer your primary residence. This prospect raises some disturbing questions: What if your neighborhood goes downhill, or your children move across the country and you no longer have ties to the area? What if you require an assisted-living situation or otherwise need long-term care outside your home?

While the bank can't kick you out or tap any assets beyond your residence itself, the moment that you sell for any reason, they'll take their money back. That cash is gone forever and won't be available to make the down payment on a new house somewhere else, or be put toward any other purpose. Even if you still have enough left for another down payment, you won't be eligible for a conventional mortgage elsewhere unless you also have a regular paycheck (although combined with a reverse mortgage on your new house, it might be enough to purchase it outright).

In Closing

There is a lot of information out there to help you make a decision about reverse mortgages. The AARP is all over these loans and has an extensive discussion of them on its Website: **www.aarp.org/rev mort**. It makes available unbiased counselors and even offers an online calculator that will lead you through exactly what to expect in terms of costs and gains.

The AARP Website is a good first stop for the reverse-mortgage shopper. Additionally, a calculator that will allow you to compare what you might get from the HECM, Fannie Mae, and private-reverse-mortgage lenders can be found at **www.financialfreedom.com**. To find a financial institution offering a federally insured HECM loan, you can go to **www.hud.gov/ll/code/llplcrit.html** and punch in your city.

■ ■ ■

Afterword

We've given you the tools that you need to financially plan your retirement. The next step is for you to take charge of your finances, and do it today—right now, this minute. You know that shoe box full of old papers and the file folder with all those statements you couldn't bear to look at that you thought you might get to someday? That day is today. Get them out right now and start going through them. Once you take a fearless inventory of your financial situation, you'll be amazed by how much the rest of your life falls into line.

Figure out what you're earning, spending, and saving. If you're like nearly everyone else, you're probably not saving enough. While it's said that misery loves company, you won't want to be sitting next to the miserable souls in the soup kitchen when you're 75. Or, as William Bernstein's mother, Lilian, used to tell him: "Money doesn't buy happiness, but at least you can suffer in comfort."

Use our Website (**www.stein-demuth.com**), and make the best estimates that you can as to where you stand with regard to your retirement savings. What you don't know *can* hurt you—and what you do know will make you strong. Even if the news looks terrible, it's better to know it now, when you can still take action, than to find out when you're 70 and less employable, with less time to do anything about it.

Start saving more, preferably through automatic deposits from your paycheck straight to Vanguard, Fidelity, or T. Rowe Price. Those credit cards? Pay off your balances in their entirety every month. And keep the same car in your driveway for eight or ten years.

Take charge, because you're your own rescue party right now—and until you retire, and then after that. To paraphrase Winston Churchill: We offer you the tools, but *you* have to finish the job.

■ ■ ■

APPENDIX

25 Big Truths of Retirement Planning

1. **There's no Lone Ranger coming to rescue the baby boomers and Gen Xers.** There isn't enough money anywhere to foot the bill—not in Social Security and Medicare, nor in your pension plans or personal savings. The U.S. taxpayers in aggregate cannot tax themselves into solvency.

2. **If you want to retire, you're going to have to save yourself.** If you're old enough to have sex, you're old enough to be saving for your retirement.

3. **You have to start saving early.** This will let the power of compound interest do all the heavy lifting. If you wait, you'll have to do it by the brute force of self-denial. Wait still longer and it won't be possible to retire at all.

4. It's vastly more important that you **hit upon a pretty good investment plan and save regularly** than that you find the perfect, brilliant investment plan and save haphazardly.

5. **It's very difficult to beat the couch potato portfolio:** 50 percent total stock market index, 50 percent total bond market index.

6. **People with savings will end up at a tremendous advantage over those without.** This latter, struggling

group may end up including many of your friends.

7.   **Don't postpone planning your retirement,** since doing so is, in effect, to have already made the decision about where you're headed. Hint: It's not Millionaire Estates.

8.   The X-factor of unknown future tax rates, as well as the tenuousness of Social Security and Medicare, make it exceedingly difficult to plan accurately. Everything points to the need to **err on the side of oversaving.**

9.   **If you want a guarantee, buy a toaster.**

10. You have to **get off the high-consumption treadmill, maximize your human capital, and plan to work as long as possible** (preferably into retirement, at least part-time).

11. **You'll be paying for the bulk of retirement yourself** out of your personal savings.

12. **Those who have saved will be made to pay for those who haven't.** Unfortunately, this means that you need to save even more.

13. **The upper-middle class will be the hardest hit of all.** They'll likely see nothing from Social Security and little from Medicare; meanwhile, the IRS will turn them upside down and shake them by the ankles to get the money to pay for everyone else. With their vastly insufficient savings, their lifestyles are going to shrink like an Armani suit in the dryer.

14. If you're a high-income type, don't use a self-help book or a Website calculator to plan your retirement. **Get the professional help you need,** preferably sooner rather than later. A fee-based Certified Financial Planner with expertise

in the area of retirement planning is a good place to start.

15.   You'll need private savings equal to 15 to 20 times the annual income you need to replace, which will typically be about 80 percent of your pre-retirement salary. In other words, **you'll need 12 to 16 times your final salary to maintain something like your standard of living,** assuming that you have no pension or Social Security, and that you'll receive historical investment returns going forward.

16.   **You need to plan for your** *maximum* **life span,** not your *average* life span. There's a 5 percent chance that you'll live to be 100, and a one percent chance that you'll live to be 105.

17.   Investment returns going forward from current valuation levels may well be lower than they were during the boom times of the 20th century. **Being a long-term investor doesn't mean that you'll get historical rates of return.**

18.   **You can't figure this out once and for all.** You have to monitor your progress and make midcourse corrections.

19.   **New retirees are long-term investors:** If they go too conservative, they run out of money later. That said, early retirement is by far the most dangerous time for your investments.

20.   **The advantage conferred by dollar cost averaging** over the years on the savings side is directly handed back during retirement by *negative* dollar cost averaging on the withdrawal side.

21.   **Long-term market timing** can add value to your savings as well as your withdrawals, so value the market before buying or selling. This is the cure for negative dollar cost averaging.

22. **Don't put all of your savings into one type of account,** be it an IRA, a Keogh, a taxable account, or any other vehicle. Who knows where the tax man's heaviest hand will fall in the future?

23. This is nature's cruel joke on retirees: **You'll probably have a lot of money later, when you can't spend it, but you only get a pittance early on in retirement when you could really use it.** Thus, the problem: How do we bring Oz back to Kansas? How do we siphon the money from the account in Tomorrowland to our bank on Main Street today?

24. **After you retire, you have to recalculate your with-drawal rate periodically.** If your portfolio is down 10 percent in the first few years, cut back your withdrawals to a relatively safe 4 percent initial withdrawal rate, no matter what the calculators say.

25. If you don't have enough, you can still find a way to live comfortably during retirement through these options: **Use your savings to purchase immediate annuities, relocate to an area with a lower cost of living, and take out a reverse mortgage,** or some combination of these.

■ ■ ■

Retirement Withdrawal Strategies—Other Voices

Your authors aren't the first, and certainly won't be the last, to devise stratagems for safely and efficiently drawing down a nest egg. This portion of the book presents a few other points of view on the topic, along with our highly biased annotations.

A Brief Overview of Contemporary
Retirement Withdrawal Discoveries

In Chapter 6, we mentioned that Fidelity Magellan Fund helmsman Peter Lynch, in his book *Beating the Street,* suggested that retirees could withdraw 7 percent annually from their 100 percent stock portfolio—a recommendation that he also repeated in his September 1995 *Worth* magazine article "Fear of Crashing." This turned out to be overly optimistic. Just because the 10.6 percent average returns from the stock market are higher than his figure doesn't mean that you'll get those average returns every year. A few bad years up front and your funds will quickly be exhausted at this withdrawal rate. Columnist Scott Burns of *The Dallas Morning News* pointed out that on at least one occasion since 1960, this portfolio would have been depleted in as few as 15 years.

Of course, Lynch was correct in his insight that there's *some* percentage from a total stock portfolio that will be a sustainable withdrawal rate. He just overshot the mark by a wide margin—possibly due to his own tremendously successful record as an investor.

Thus, one of the first big insights was that retirement withdrawals from a portfolio of stocks and bonds can't be estimated using straight-line growth rates, as are assumed by the ubiquitous "retirement planner" applets found on the Internet (and until recently, even on the Websites of respected financial-service institutions who should have known better). The variability of stock- and bond-market returns and the uncertain sequence that they come in mean that you have to withdraw significantly less in order to avoid getting wiped out by an unlucky streak early in your retirement. It's not the returns that kill you, it's their standard deviation.

In 1994, William Bengen wrote an important article calculating that given an annually rebalanced 50 percent stock/50 percent bond portfolio, the maximum safe-withdrawal rate was 4 percent of the portfolio's initial value, adjusted for inflation annually thereafter, when stretched over a 30-year retirement. Bengen was writing in response to a *Money* magazine article suggesting that 5.29 percent was a safe initial-withdrawal rate, but his experience was different than the article's author: At the higher rate, he found several historical sequences that had retirees running out of money, and in one case, this happened in only 18 years.

Basing his data on the actual returns of the market indexes since 1926, he recommended a portfolio of closer to 75 percent stocks and 25 percent bonds, with the caveat that it could do far worse in bad times (but far better in good) than a 50-50 portfolio. Bengen's finding sent a shudder through the financial-planning world, as the idea dawned that a lot of people didn't have enough savings to retire.

Then in 1998, Philip L. Cooley, Carl M. Hubbard, and Daniel T. Walz, professors of finance in the department of business administration at Trinity University in San Antonio, Texas, published the eponymous "Trinity Study," which looked at sustainable withdrawal rates from various asset allocations for the historical period from 1926 to 1995. They found that a 50 percent stock/50 percent bond portfolio would have sustained a 4 percent annual withdrawal rate, adjusted for inflation every 12 months, over about 95 percent of the rolling 30-year periods. This was picked up by the press and caused a large collective gulp on the part of the baby boomers. However, their pain was temporarily mollified by the influence of the NASDAQ bubble, which promised to make everyone into instant millionaires.

In 2002, Gordon Pye, writing in *The Journal of Portfolio Management,* applied Monte Carlo methodology to the question of sustainable withdrawal rates. This large technological advance nonetheless came to similar conclusions as those who had studied the historical record alone: The 4 percent initial-withdrawal rate still seemed the prudent, sustainable decision.

Zvi Bodie, professor of finance and economics at the Boston University School of Management, holds the contrarian opinion that stocks are generally too risky for retirees because of the unwarranted assumption that retired persons' investments will match the average stock market historical returns. Bodie wants to fund retirement accounts primarily with inflation-indexed bonds, both on the saving and distribution side. Obviously, such a conservative approach requires substantially more assets: At recent auctions, ten-year inflation-indexed bonds have yielded a real 2 percent annually. This means that you would need 50 times your current self-generated income to lock in your retirement.

The deep thinkers in the field have all been grappling with one central problem: If you want to withdraw a fixed amount of money every year and adjust it for inflation to keep your purchasing power constant, then how can you avoid having to sell a lot of stocks (which you need for growth) early on if the market is down? We've put a few of the more popular strategies up against one another to see how well they fare.

191

The Big Withdrawal Grudge Match

In a maneuver guaranteed to infuriate everyone, your authors have jury-rigged an experiment to examine how some of these different methods might have worked for someone retiring for 30 years with $1 million in January 1929—the year the Great Depression began. Remember what we said about early losses being the worst for retirees? This time period gives us that problem in spades.

We freely concede that we aren't *exactly* duplicating anyone's model, including our own. But we've tried to get into the spirit of each approach to see how it fared, and we'll note the many shortcomings of our experiment as we go along. We apologize in advance to anyone whose ideas we've inadvertently given short shrift. Look at it this way: It will give the annoyed researchers an excuse to write an article (possibly a review?) berating us. Keep in mind that no allowance has been made in any of these trial runs for taxes, transaction costs, or management fees.

The Omega Strategy

In December 2000, financial columnist Scott Burns suggested the "Omega" strategy, which makes a lot of sense, just like everything he writes. He didn't quantify it or provide a historical analysis, but the tune goes like this: During years when the stock market is up, make your retirement withdrawals from the stock market side of your portfolio; in the years that it's down, pull from your bonds instead.

Astute readers will see that this is similar to our market-timing strategy, except that Burns's withdrawals are based on the current one-year total returns from the stock market, not its longer-term valuation. The big idea here is to use bonds as a buffer in order to prevent you from selling your stocks when they're down (and Burns goes the further step of recommending a bond portfolio of Treasury Inflation-Protected Securities or I bonds). This gives your stock portfolio a chance to recover and fight another day.

Our 1929 to 1959 poor-man's test of the Omega strategy didn't use inflation-indexed bonds because they didn't exist in 1929. Instead, we patched together a 1929 "Model T" couch potato portfolio using a mix of the total stock market (deciles 1 to 10 as given by the Center for Research in Securities Prices) and long-term government bonds on the bond side—which ends up having a much longer maturity and higher credit quality than the Lehman Brothers Aggregate does today.

Then we took the generic 4 percent withdrawal rate as our starting point ($40,000), adjusting it for inflation every year thereafter. On years when stocks were up, we sold from the stock side of the portfolio; when stocks were down, we withdrew from the bond side. Figure A.1 shows the score.

Figure A.1: Faux-Omega Strategy

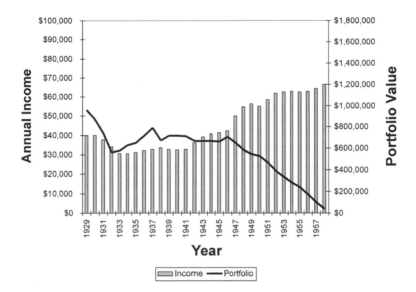

Since we're going to show you a number of similar charts, you might as well pause for a moment to get your bearings. The left-hand scale is the annual income that the strategy produces, which is shown in the columns that follow. The right-hand scale gives the total value of the portfolio over time, corresponding to the black line on the chart. In both cases, higher is better. When comparing two charts, make sure you note whether the axes are scaled the same way.

As you look over these figures, pay special attention to any spots where one of the columns shows your income dropping from year to year—that's what hurts. If your income is steady, that's fine; and if it's rising, well, this is a problem we'd all like to have. In Figure A.1, the income is actually constant throughout the entire period in terms of purchasing power, because it's adjusted annually for inflation.

Here's our postgame analysis: While Omega correctly didn't touch the stocks when they were in free fall during the opening years of the Depression, the strategy was there with its hand out as soon as the stocks made some fledgling efforts to crawl back, tapping them for the full tariff. This wiped out the stock side of our portfolio in year 19. We could have stopped the madness by rebalancing the portfolio, but that violated the idea of selling stocks only when they'd been up for the year.

After we ran out of stocks, we lived off of our bonds from years 20 to 30. The portfolio successfully kept a steady inflation-adjusted $40,000 coming throughout our retirement, allowing us to pull out $1,222,196 in all, and leaving us with $40,304 in bonds in the end . . . we would not have lasted one more year at this rate.

In hindsight, the portfolio would have worked far better had we rebalanced at some gross threshold—say, when it became lopsided 25 percent/75 percent one way or the other, or just selling evenly from both the stock and bond sides would have left us with the identical income stream, but a final account worth $266,336 (since the stocks would have had more room to grow).

While this doesn't mean that selling when the market is up for the year is a bad strategy in general, it certainly would have worked against you if you'd the misfortune to retire in 1929. The great virtue of the 4 percent withdrawal rate is that your purchasing power remains steady throughout your retirement; the disadvantage is that you might be able to do better.

The Galeno Strategy

A number of experts have recommend putting several years' worth of total-initial savings in cash (say, five years' worth) and drawing down a fixed percentage (such as 1/60th) from this cash buffer every month. Then you replenish with periodic stock-market sales (perhaps selling 4 percent of your stock portfolio every January). This is known as the "Galeno" strategy after the person who proposed it in the Internet chat rooms where such ideas are fervently discussed. The premise is to use cash (or money-market funds, short-term bonds, or ladders of Treasury bonds or CDs) as the insulation from stock-market downturns.

Note: A highly intelligent, well-thought-out relative of the Galeno strategy is the *Buckets of Money* plan described in the book by that name, authored by Raymond J. Lucia (who also has a Website and a national radio program). His basic idea is to take your money and put it into "buckets" to get ready (in the late phase) for your retirement: One bucket has conservatively chosen long-term investments, such as broad stock market indexes; another might have more careful investments such as medium-term bonds. The first bucket would have very liquid investments such as money market funds—or even cash.

The general idea is that the investor has the buckets of liquid assets to draw upon so that the long-term investments can increase and only be drawn upon after they've grown substantially in value. This is so that the longer-term investments can pass through ups and downs—usually ups—and grow without being disturbed during down periods.

They say that great ideas are often basic, and this uncomplicated one has quite a bit of merit. Lucia says that it helps to think of retirement as a large liability that has to be met with adequate assets— another simple idea, but utterly compelling, and one that tells the truth of the retirement story.

One of your authors, Ben Stein, plans to speak at conferences sponsored by Lucia and has a business relationship with him. We hope that you won't let our bias keep you from heeding his sound precepts.

195

To resume: We were able to approximate the Galeno strategy pretty closely by putting our stocks in the total stock market portfolio (as we described earlier) and putting our cash in T-bills. Figure A.2 (page 196) shows the results of following this method.

Figure A.2: Faux-Galeno Strategy

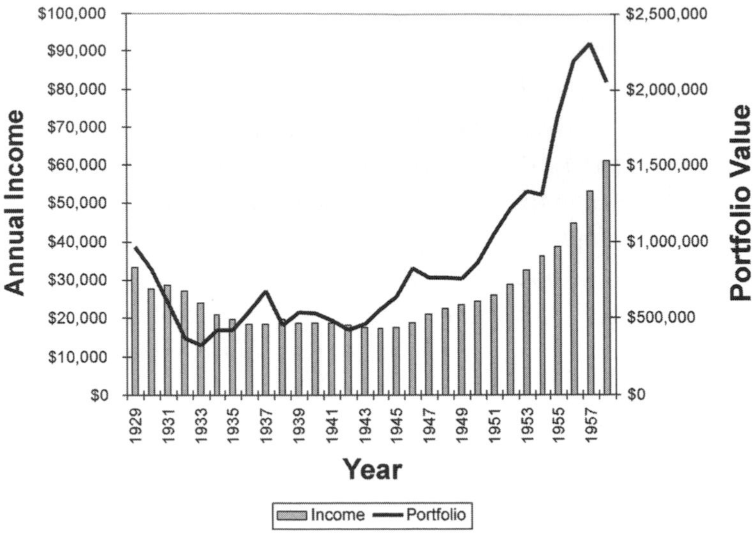

The Galeno strategy got us through the Great Depression but may be faulted for being too conservative. Selling 4 percent of our 100 percent stock portfolio when stocks were down led to a steadily shrinking cash account, and in turn to a steadily lowering take-home paycheck. These low initial withdrawals led to a big portfolio in the end but didn't do a good job of optimizing our cash flow in early retirement. More portfolio diversification (that is, bonds) might have helped as well. This strategy seems to be best suited to investors with large estates who have sizable bequest motives and are able to live off a small fraction of their total savings.

The Grangaard Strategy

Financial analyst Paul Grangaard has tried a different version of this approach. He recommends that you consider selling half of your diversified-stock portfolio at the outset of retirement in order to purchase a ten-year ladder of fixed-income investments such as Treasury notes or bank CDs (or even zero coupon bonds). As these mature every year, you'll live off this certain income for the decade.

Then starting with year 11, you'll sell half of your stock portfolio once more (which has been growing this whole time) and buy another ten-year fixed-income ladder . . . and so on for every following decade. The premise is that the luxury of time allows your stocks to grow and replenish (and more) whatever was lost in the starting disbursement.

We tried putting this to the test as best we could with our 1929 to 1959 data. Grangaard sensibly recommends using a more diversified stock portfolio than our total U.S. stock market, although it's questionable whether adding asset classes would have improved the results materially in the midst of a global depression.

We sold half of the portfolio on day one and (artificially) constructed bond ladders to meet our income needs for the next decade; then we did the same thing for 1939 and 1949. The results are shown in Figure A.3.

Figure A.3: Faux-Grangaard Strategy

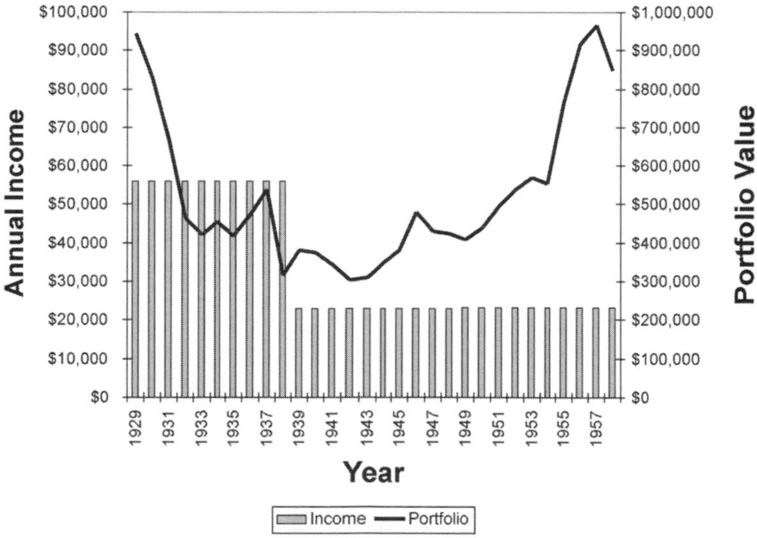

We were killed by bad timing. After selling half of our stocks and putting them into a bond ladder from 1929 to 1939 (allowing us to collect a rock-solid $56,101 per year throughout the Great Depression), suddenly our bond ladders ran out in 1939 and it was time to sell half our stocks again in order to build a new one. Only now, our stocks were worth . . . a meager $315,635. This new bond ladder gave us $22,800, a 60 percent pay cut. In 1949 the strategy worked as intended, thanks to the stock-market recovery in the 1940s, and we got a raise to $23,069—but that's too little, too late.

Paul Grangaard is a smart guy, and we certainly don't mean to imply that investors following his method are headed for a fall. We only want to point out that this iteration of his strategy didn't seem to work very well during the Great Depression.

The Gummy Strategy

Here's another variation: Sell a higher percentage of your stocks after an "up" market year and a lower percentage after a "down" year. This is the "Gummy" solution, named for the sobriquet of the retired math teacher who proposed it on the Internet. Instead of withdrawing the safe 4 percent from your portfolio for year one and adjusting this amount for inflation thereafter, you'll withdraw 3 percent the first year, plus 50 percent of anything that the market returns above the rate of inflation.

This means that you'll accept a lower "floor" (or basic starting income), but have a higher "ceiling," potentially letting you extract more cash from your portfolio over your entire retirement. In effect, you get a joyride during the good times.

Gummy proposed using a "slice and dice" portfolio consisting of equal parts large-cap-growth, large-cap-value, small-cap-growth, and small-cap-value stocks. While our total stock market includes all of these, the returns aren't exactly the same as Gummy's 4 x 25 (that is, the four types of stocks, each making up 25 percent of the account) portfolio would have accrued. Still, it's doubtful that the Gummy option would have performed significantly better over this dismal period.

Unfortunately, you see, this portfolio was doomed from year one, because in 1928, the stock market was up 38.7 percent, while inflation was −.98 percent. Pocketing half of this overage for extra spending money made for an excessively generous first-year paycheck of $228,300—the very antithesis of prudent retirement management. Then the Great Depression hit in 1929, and our income in year two drops to $30,063. After that, the portfolio limps along for 23 more years before going bust, as Figure A.4 attests.

Figure A.4: Faux-Gummy Strategy

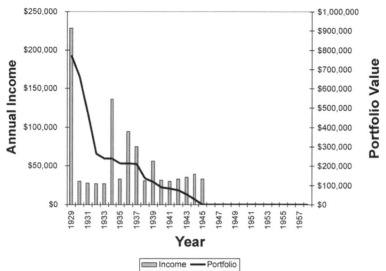

In retrospect, it's clear that the stock market was too wild to let us take home even half of such a large gain. If we capped our windfalls at one-quarter of any inflation-beating overage, the portfolio lasted for 30 years, but the jumps in income from year to year were still disconcerting, often rising or falling $30,000 at a pop (see Figure A.5, page 200). We love Gummy, but this particular proposal seems to have limitations.

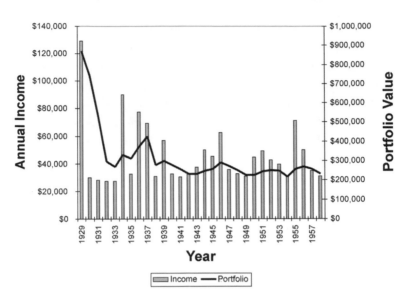

Figure A.5: Faux-Modified-Gummy Strategy

The Guyton Strategy

Recently, Certified Financial Planner Jonathan Guyton did an elaborate series of data-mining experiments, spelunking through a terrible period of stock-market returns for his analysis of the years 1973 to 2003. He tweaked his findings until he came up with a way to safely withdraw an initial 5.8 to 6.2 percent.

In hindsight, there were three keys to achieving his results:

1. Sell any excess over the targeted allocation every year and keep the proceeds in a cash account, always drawing from this first (then from bonds and finally from stocks, if necessary).

2. Don't allow an increase in the withdrawal following any year when the portfolio's total return was negative.

3. Cap an inflation cost-of-living allowance on withdrawals at 6 percent per year, with no makeup for any shortfall thereafter.

Guyton is so impressed with his findings that he says he's applied for a patent on them! Perhaps he plans sell them to Parker Brothers for a board game?

He used a bunch of asset classes that were unavailable in 1929, so we'll use the entire U.S. stock market as a proxy. Since the Depression was global, and international stocks were hit just as hard as domestic ones (as was real estate), we question whether an even more diversified portfolio would have made much difference. We used long-term government bonds for his bond fund and T-bills for his cash account.

In trying to get into the Guyton spirit, we started by withdrawing 5.3 percent, picking a rate substantially lower than that promised by his 1973 to 2003 sample. We then divided the money into 65 percent stocks and 35 percent bonds. We put any winnings past the 65 percent stock allocation into the T-bill account and used that first to cover our annual income requirement; thereafter we went to bonds, and only then to stocks.

We tried (but ultimately failed) to never withdraw from an asset class that had a down year. We never increased our withdrawal amount during any year when the portfolio fell in value, and when we did increase it, we only did so by the amount of inflation that particular year (the 6 percent inflation-adjustment limit never was invoked).

With all of these rules in play, we still ran out of money after 19 years. The withdrawal rate was just too high for the overweight stock portfolio to sustain during a decade when stocks got put through the Vegematic. Selling stocks to maintain the portfolio's allocation and parking the cash in T-bills may be a great strategy when inflation is rampant and T-bills are paying over 10 percent (as they did in the 1970s), but during the Depression, their rates were low and all this selling of stocks when they were cheap proved disastrous, as Figure A.6 (page 202) shows.

Figure A.6: Faux-Guyton 65% Stock Strategy

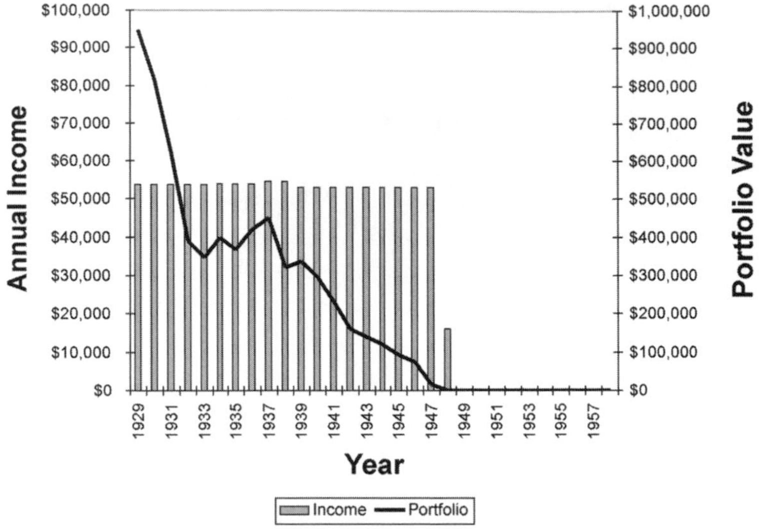

We tried the Guyton rules one more time, in this case using his 80 percent stock/20 percent bond allocation and lowering the initial-withdrawal rate to 5 percent. Things went even worse with this scenario, and this time the portfolio only lasted 17 years. A big stock position was a bad idea in 1929, as you can see in Figure A.7.

Figure A.7: Faux-Guyton 80% Stock Strategy

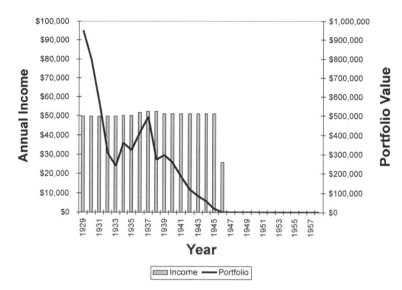

While this back testing is suggestive rather than definitive, it leads us to the suspect that this strategy needs some fine-tuning before it's widely marketed. Coming up with a perfect solution for one time period often fails upon cross-validation, and it appears that may be the case here.

The Stein-DeMuth Strategy

To test our version, we used the same "Model T" couch potato portfolio consisting of the total stock market and long-term government bonds. We tried our 99 percent safe-withdrawal rates, taking out 5.3 percent as our initial-withdrawal rate for the first five years, adjusting for inflation (that is, 5.6 percent for the second five years, and so on). We took a few of the precautions that we've recommended throughout the book, although none of them proved necessary.

After the market crashed in 1929, we cut our withdrawal rate to 4 percent of the initial portfolio (adjusting for inflation from years three to five). We rebalanced every year for the first five years, because we knew that these were perilous times (to put it mildly); otherwise, we only rebalanced our 50-50 portfolio when it was out of tolerance more than 60/40 or 40/60. Finally, during the last ten years, we dropped back to the 100 percent safe-withdrawal rate of 8.6 percent.

On the sell side, we unloaded 75 percent from the stock side when stocks looked overvalued to us, and 75 percent from the bond side when they appeared undervalued, per our market-valuation approach. The results are shown in Figure A.8.

Figure A.8: Faux-Stein-DeMuth 99% Safe Strategy

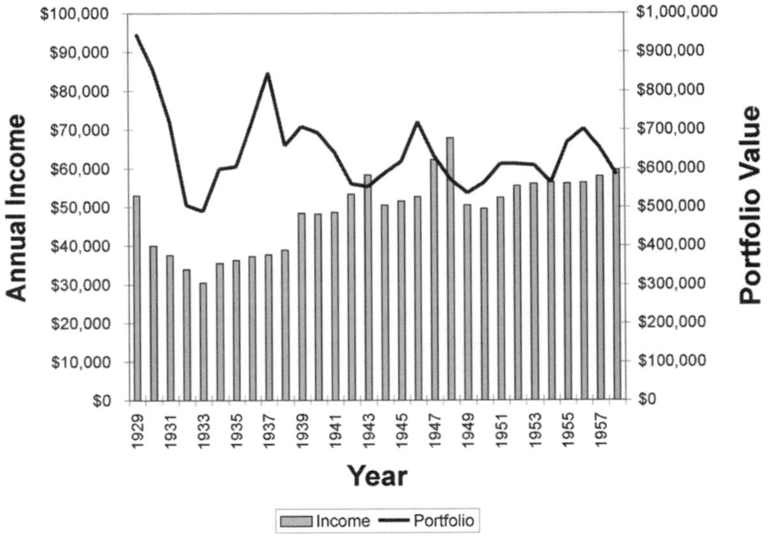

Emboldened by our success, we tried plugging in our 95 percent safe-portfolio-withdrawal rates: We took 6.2 percent out the first year, adjusting this for inflation even as the market collapsed all around us for years two through five, then bumping it up to 6.6 percent for years six through ten, and so on.

Unbelievably, the portfolio held. We took no safe harbor at 4 percent when the Great Depression hit, and we continued to take withdrawals at the 95 percent success rate during the final decade. Take a look at the results as shown in Figure A.9.

Figure A.9: Faux-Stein-DeMuth 95% Safe Strategy

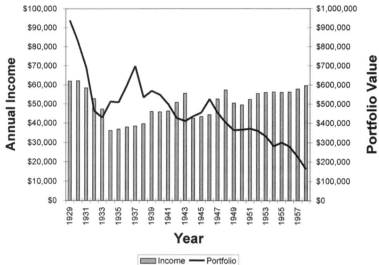

205

Our much-vaunted market-timing sell strategy didn't add much value over this period. The real hero was the Monte Carlo stress testing, which anticipated the tough times ahead and kept us safe even at higher withdrawal rates than most previous studies have advocated.

What about 1973 to 2003? Just to be sure, we also ran the Stein-DeMuth withdrawal rates over the other excrutiating period for retirement during the last century: starting in 1973, just before rampant inflation hit the stock and bond markets. Our results are shown in Figures A.10 and A.11 (page 206).

Figure A.10: Stein-DeMuth 99% Safe Strategy 1973–2003

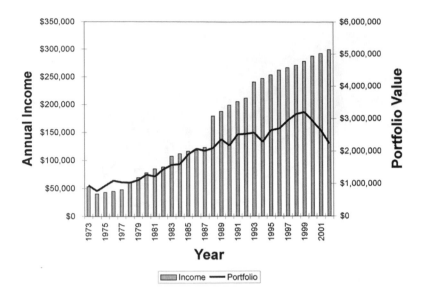

Figure A.11: Stein-DeMuth 95% Safe Strategy 1973–2003

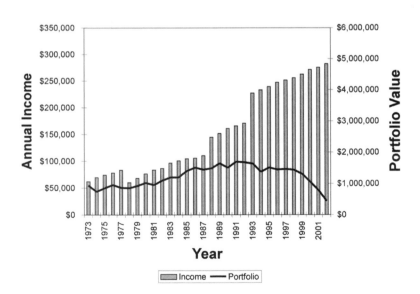

Once again, both portfolio withdrawal rates saw us through. We used the standard safety precautions for the 99 percent safe run, and none for the 95 percent safe run. Here market-timing our withdrawals added some value over pulling evenly from both sides of the portfolio. Once again, even at the riskier 95 percent safe withdrawal level, our portfolio held.

■

In sum, Table A.1 shows how the more successful approaches stacked up during times that were bound to try any strategy's mettle. It details the average income that an investor would have gleaned for each decade of this 30-year retirement, starting in 1929 and following our admittedly corrupt (but sincerely motivated) attempt to reconstitute these approaches with the resources available back then. It also shows the biggest one-year drop in income that would have jolted the retiree and the final value of their account in 1959. Note that these are nominal values (not adjusted for inflation).

Table A.1: Successful Income Withdrawal Strategy Comparisons 1929-1958

Strategy	Early Rtrmnt.	Middle Rtrmnt.	Late Rtrmnt.	Biggest 1-Year Drop	Final Estate
Omega	$34,315	$40,372	$61,334	$3,586	$40,304
Galeno	$23,909	$18,977	$36,947	$5,403	$2,049,413
Stein-DeMuth 99% Safe	$38,088	$54,197	$55,080	$13,000	$584,505
Stein-DeMuth 95% Safe	$47,218	$48,538	$55,037	$11,191	$163,463
Grangaard	$56,101	$22,800	$23,069	$33,301	$848,891

Perhaps the best baseline for comparison would be a generic 4 percent withdrawal rate, adjusted for inflation thereafter, while drawing down from the stock and bond sides of the portfolio evenly every year. This would have allowed you to harvest $1.2 million from your million-dollar account starting in 1929 (a real $40,000 per year for 30 years), and left you at the end of 1958 with an estate worth $160,247 (in 1929 dollars).

The Stein-DeMuth "99 percent safe" strategy would have allowed you to pull $1,346,624 from your account over this same period, and your estate would have been worth $351,681.

The Stein-DeMuth "95 percent safe" strategy would have let you take $1,395,629 over the 30 years, leaving a final estate of $98,351 (as taking more money up front led to less money later on). Again, all these are inflation-adjusted 1929 dollars.

Although we have been examining one historical horrible-case scenario, the trade-off that it illustrates is enduring: Accepting a fluctuating income stream lets you pull out more money overall—in this case, about 11 percent more. Your mileage may vary.

■ ■ ■

Index

The letters *f* and *t* following page numbers refer to figures and tables respectively.

■ ■ ■

About the Authors

Ben Stein can be seen talking about finance on Fox TV news every week and writing about it regularly in *The New York Times* Sunday Business Section. No wonder: Not only is he the son of the world-famous economist and government adviser Herbert Stein, but Ben is a respected economist in his own right. He received his B.A. with honors in economics from Columbia University in 1966, studied economics in the graduate school of economics at Yale while he earned his law degree there, and worked as an economist for the Department of Commerce.

Ben Stein is known to many as a movie and television personality, especially from *Ferris Bueller's Day Off* and from his long-running quiz show, *Win Ben Stein's Money.* But he has probably worked more in personal and corporate finance than anything else. He has written about finance for *Barron's* and *The Wall Street Journal* for decades. He was one of the chief busters of the junk-bond frauds of the 1980s, has been a long-time critic of corporate executives' self-dealing, and has written three self-help books about personal finance. He frequently travels the country, speaking about finance in both serious and humorous ways. He is the honorary chair of the National Retirement Planning Coalition.

Website: **www.benstein.com**

Phil DeMuth was the valedictorian of his class at the University of California at Santa Barbara in 1972, then took his master's in communications and Ph.D. in clinical psychology. Both a psychologist and registered investment adviser, Phil has written for *The Wall Street Journal, Barron's,* the *Louis Rukeyser Newsletter,* and **forbes.com**, as well as *Human Behavior* and *Psychology Today.* His opinions have been quoted in **theStreet.com**, *On Wall Street,* and *Fortune* magazine, and he has been profiled in *Research* magazine and seen on *Forbes on Fox* and *Wall Street Week.* He is president of Conservative Wealth Management in Los Angeles, a registered investment counsel to high-net-worth individuals and their families.

Website: **www.phildemuth.com**

■ ■ ■

Financial Notes

Financial Notes

Financial Notes

Financial Notes

■ ■ ■

NBP

We hope you enjoyed this book.
If you'd like additional information, please contact
New Beginnings Press through their distributors:

Hay House, Inc.
P.O. Box 5100
Carlsbad, CA 92018-5100

(760) 431-7695 or (800) 654-5126
(760) 431-6948 (fax) or (800) 650-5115 (fax)
www.hayhouse.com®

■ ■ ■

Distributed in Australia by:
Hay House Australia Pty. Ltd., 18/36 Ralph St., Alexandria NSW 2015
Phone: 612-9669-4299 • Fax: 612-9669-4144 • www.hayhouse.com.au

Distributed in the United Kingdom by:
Hay House UK, Ltd., 292B Kensal Rd., London W10 5BE
Phone: 44-20-8962-1230 • Fax: 44-20-8962-1239 • www.hayhouse.co.uk

Distributed in the Republic of South Africa by:
Hay House SA (Pty), Ltd., P.O. Box 990, Witkoppen 2068
Phone/Fax: 27-11-467-8904 • orders@psdprom.co.za • www.hayhouse.co.za

Distributed in India by:
Hay House Publishers India, Muskaan Complex,
Plot No. 3, B-2, Vasant Kunj, New Delhi 110 070 • Phone: 91-11-4176-1620
Fax: 91-11-4176-1630 • www.hayhouse.co.in

Distributed in Canada by:
Raincoast, 9050 Shaughnessy St., Vancouver, B.C. V6P 6E5
Phone: (604) 323-7100 • Fax: (604) 323-2600 • www.raincoast.com

■ ■ ■

Tune in to **HayHouseRadio.com**® for the best in inspirational talk radio
featuring top Hay House authors! And, sign up via the Hay House USA
Website to receive the Hay House online newsletter and stay informed
about what's going on with your favorite authors. You'll receive
bimonthly announcements about: Discounts and Offers, Special Events,
Product Highlights, Free Excerpts, Giveaways, and more!
www.hayhouse.com®